Shakes... Educa...

Edited by

Martin Blocksidge

continuum
LONDON • NEW YORK

Continuum
The Tower Building
11 York Road
London SE1 7NX

15 East 26th Street
New York
NY 10010

www.continuumbooks.com

First published 2003 by Continuum
This paperback edition published 2005
© Martin Blocksidge 2003

British Library Cataloguing-in-Publication Data
A catalogue record for this book is available from the British Library

ISBN 0–8264–5433–X (hardback)
    0–8264–8574–X (paperback)

Typeset by Kenneth Burnley, Wirral, Cheshire
Printed and bound in Great Britain by
Antony Rowe Ltd., Chippenham, Wiltshire.

Contents

Notes on contributors

Catherine Alexander is Lecturer in Shakespeare Studies at the Shakespeare Birthplace Trust in Stratford-on-Avon, Honorary Research Fellow at the University of Birmingham and a visiting lecturer at Birmingham and Cambridge Universities. She is editor of *Shakespeare and Language* and co-editor with Stanley Wells of *Shakespeare and Race* and *Shakespeare and Sexuality* (both published by Cambridge University Press). Catherine is also co-editor of *The Cambridge Bibliography of English Literature*, Volume 2, and editor of *The Cambridge Shakespeare Library* and *Bibliotecha Georgiana*. Currently working on an edition of Elizabeth Montagu's letters, she is Executive Secretary of the International Shakespeare Association and an Executive Member of the English Association.

Martin Blocksidge is currently President of the English Association. He taught English in schools for 30 years and is now involved in work with trainee teachers and on the provision of INSET courses. He edited *Teaching Literature 11–18* (2000) and has written a study of Pope's satire, as well as articles on nineteenth-century poetry, on Shakespeare and on aspects of English teaching.

Joseph Francis teaches English at Eton College, having previously taught at Tonbridge School. He studied at Oxford University and at the University of Mississippi, and has taught English as a foreign language in Italy. He has worked as an examiner at both GCSE and A-level. He writes poetry, fiction and criticism, and won the Keats–Shelley Memorial Essay Prize in 2002. Joseph regularly directs student theatre and has helped bring new writing from students to the stage.

Sue Gregory has many years of experience in teaching English. Formerly Head of English at Gartree High School, Leicester, she is now a freelance writer. In the 1980s she produced fiction for children, including *Martini on the Rocks* and *Kill-a-Louse Week*, both published by Puffin Books. She has also written for Radio 4's *Morning Story*. Her most recent publication, written with Richard Gill, is *Mastering the Novels of Jane Austen* (Palgrave Master Series).

Elaine Harris studied at Homerton and Newnham Colleges in Cambridge. She has taught English for over 25 years in three different comprehensive schools in the West Essex area. In 1995 she became Head of English at Burnt Mill school in Harlow and soon afterwards joined the Secondary Committee of the English Association. In recent years Elaine has helped to organize conferences and been a regular reviewer for *The Use of English* and for Longmans. In 2000 she took a year's sabbatical and returned to full-time study at Queen Mary College, London, where she took a master's degree in eighteenth-century English Literature.

Sean McEvoy is English Area Co-ordinator at Varndean College, Brighton. He also teaches at the University of Sussex and on the Shakespeare MA course at Royal Holloway

College, London, where he is also completing a Ph.D. thesis on Ben Jonson. He is the author of *Shakespeare: The Basics* (Routledge, 2000) and the forthcoming Routledge Literary Sourcebook on *Hamlet*.

Tiffany Stern is a Senior Lecturer at Oxford Brookes University and is author of *Rehearsal from Shakespeare to Sheridan* (Oxford University Press, 2000), and editor of the anonymous *King Leir* (Nick Hern Books, 2002). She is currently editing Sheridan's *The Rivals* for the New Mermaid series, and writing a book, *Making Shakespeare,* to be published in Routledge's Accents on Shakespeare series. She is, with Simon Palfrey, co-writing a third book, *Shakespeare in Parts*, and has published numerous articles and chapters on Shakespeare and his theatre.

Editor's note

In 2000, I edited and contributed to a volume of essays called *Teaching Literature 11–18*. It was a conscious editorial policy in commissioning those essays to exclude any discussion of teaching Shakespeare. This was not done for any sinister ideological reason, but because it was felt that the teaching of Shakespeare was a suitable subject for a whole book.

This book both is and is not a sequel to *Teaching Literature 11–18*. The structure – a collection of essays by experienced practitioners – is similar, but its emphasis is different. Whilst neither title has been conceived as a guidebook for teachers looking for practical ideas, the bent of this one is more philosophical. It seeks to define, or at least report on, the current position of Shakespeare in schools, colleges and other educational environments. Hence, whilst it might be seen as news from various parts of the frontline, its primary purpose is to examine how, where and why Shakespeare manifests himself in the educational experience of school and college students today. To change the metaphor, Shakespeare has been something of a political football in the world of education, and it now seems a good time to see where he has landed.

I should like to thank Anthony Haynes of Continuum for commissioning this book, and Alexandra Webster and

Christina Parkinson for continuing to believe in the existence of a manuscript for whose long-term invisibility I must take much of the blame.

Martin Blocksidge, December 2002

CHAPTER 1

Shakespeare:
iconic or relevant?

Martin Blocksidge

> . . . he has been separated from his fellows, and recog-
> nized for what he is: perhaps the greatest poet of all time;
> one who has said more about humanity than any other
> writer, and has said it better; whose works are the study
> and admiration of divines and philosophers, of soldiers
> and statesmen, so that his continued vogue upon the
> stage is the smallest part of his immortality; who has
> touched many spirits finely to fine issues, and has been for
> three centuries a source of delight and understanding, of
> wisdom and consolation.[1]

Thus wrote Sir Walter Raleigh in the introductory chapter to
his biography of Shakespeare, published in the *The English
Men of Letters* series in 1907. Raleigh's book was not a school
textbook: it was directed at a well-informed, conventionally
'cultured' general reader. Nevertheless, the passage which I
have just quoted bears on most of the issues which confront
anyone who thinks about the position of Shakespeare in education. For most of the twentieth century, he was indeed
'separated from his fellows'. Universities devoted whole
courses to Shakespeare with a regularity not granted to other
authors. School examination boards required A-level students

to study at least one, and normally two Shakespeare plays. Some devoted a whole paper to him: Shakespeare could constitute as much as a third of the English Literature syllabus that 16–18 year-olds followed. When the National Curriculum in English came into existence in 1990, Shakespeare was the only author compulsorily prescribed for study by all the nation's children.

Raleigh values Shakespeare 'the greatest poet' above Shakespeare the dramatist, and in so doing he is very much a child of his time. Nevertheless, our educational institutions have, on the whole, appropriated Shakespeare the poet rather than Shakespeare the dramatist. Whilst it is true that throughout the twentieth century teachers, and those who write books and articles for teachers, have issued frequent reminders that Shakespeare wrote for the theatre, and that 'active' teaching methods are likely to be the most effective in making him accessible to students, it has not been Shakespeare the playwright who has been favoured by the syllabus makers. A glance at the traditional kind of questions which A-level candidates faced shows this very clearly. On the whole, these required the students to consider Shakespeare's invention and representation of character, as if he were creating the fixed, known entities of a nineteenth-century novel. There has also been the tendency to see the plays as accretions of 'themes' or 'images', so that candidates might be encouraged to dilate on Shakespeare's presentation of good or evil, nobility, or appearance and reality, presumably on the assumption that all parties involved are agreed both on what these things are, and on what the *bien-pensant* 'bard' is telling us about them. Raleigh's 'fine issues . . . understanding . . . wisdom' are recognizable features of the examiner's Shakespeare.

Raleigh also asserts that Shakespeare has been the property of 'divines . . . philosophers . . . soldiers . . . statesmen' – not, one notices, of students. Indeed, it is difficult to imagine that Raleigh's encomium could ever much recommend its subject to the young. To use a contemporary phrase, students hardly seem to be Raleigh's target audience here: Shakespeare is definitely the property of the grown-ups.

The year before Raleigh's book was published, the English Association was founded. One of its chief aims was to propagate the subject of English, especially in schools, and in the face of the predominance of Classics which still in the minds of many educationists remained the means of providing a literary education. As Joseph Francis points out in Chapter 4 of this volume, English did not emerge as a discrete subject at Eton College until the 1960s. One of the English Association's first publications was a pamphlet which appeared in 1908 entitled 'The Teaching of Shakespeare in Schools'. Its view of Shakespeare was not markedly different from that of Raleigh, but its purpose was to persuade schools to find more room for the teaching of him. Shakespeare was knocking for admisssion to the school curriculum: 'How . . . are we to cover the ground? Above all, how are we to secure the recognition due to Shakespeare as the supreme figure of our literature?'[2] A number of methodological suggestions follow, together with an outline programme of study covering all the secondary years:

> It is desirable that all the Shakespeare chosen for study should be read aloud in class. The living voice will often give a clue to the meaning, and reading aloud is the only way of ensuring a knowledge of the metre. In a class of beginners the teacher must take a liberal share of the reading, but the pupils should be brought into play. They can be cast for some of the parts; the Forum scene in *Julius Caesar* comes one step nearer the dramatic if the

teacher is Antony and the other parts are distributed and the class is transformed into a Roman mob shouting for the will.[3]

The tone of the writing is tentative and experimental, but the suggestion that Shakespeare in the classroom benefits from some kind of 'active' teaching is noticeable. There were no drama spaces in schools in 1908, and the layout of most class-rooms would have militated against practical group work, but the shape of things to come in Shakespeare teaching can be seen here.

> The suggestion is worth considering whether it would be feasible for pupils to act in class one or more scenes from every play they study . . . In London and in large provin-cial centres it is possible to let school-children see a performance at the theatre; this plan should be encour-aged whenever it is practicable. There is a serious danger in the class-room, with text-books open before us, of our forgetting what drama really means, and burying the poet beneath a mass of comments, conundrums, and morals.[4]

Whilst this might seem little more than cautious pedagogical common sense, it is easy to forget how radical this was in 1908. The Shakespearian critic G. Wilson Knight, whose own work on Shakespeare began whilst he was employed as a schoolmaster in the 1920s, recalled that as a boy at Dulwich College before the First World War, he only ever remembered encountering one Shakespeare play. The student population of the early twenty-first century is considerably better off in this respect.

It was against this backdrop that *The Teaching of English in England*, otherwise known as the Newbolt Report, was commissioned by the government and published in 1921. It was certainly not to be the last time in the twentieth century that the government took an interest in the teaching of English; but there must be few reports that are couched in such passionate, one might almost say visionary, language.

Amongst many other matters addressed by the report was the teaching of Shakespeare: 'Shakespeare is an inevitable and necessary part of school activity because he is . . . our greatest English writer . . . Anything in our treatment that makes Shakespeare dull or distorted is a crime against his spirit.'[5] Newbolt found that the teaching of Shakespeare in elementary schools – which provided statutory education for pupils until they reached the leaving age of 13 – was patchy. In some schools, Shakespeare was widely and successfully taught; in others he was not dealt with at all. The Newbolt report, like Raleigh, was keen to stress the importance of Shakespeare both as part of a vibrant (if apocryphal) national heritage, and because he did the pupils good:

> It was in no inglorious time of our history that Englishmen delighted altogether in dance and song and drama, nor were these pleasures the privilege of a few or a class. It is a legitimate hope that a rational use of the drama in schools may bring back to England an unshamed joy in pleasures of the imagination and in the purposed expressions of wholesome and natural feeling.[6]

A member of Newbolt's committee was George Sampson, then an elementary school headmaster in London. He poured out his own hopes for the future of the subject in a book entitled *English for the English*. Sampson, too, had particular things to say about the teaching of Shakespeare. Like the authors of the English Association pamphlet, Sampson believed that

Shakespeare benefited from being read aloud in class by the teacher and that pupils should, in time, be given the opportunity to perform him: 'The sooner a child becomes familiar with the best forms of theatrical amusement the less likely is he to be permanently attracted by the worst.'[7]

Shakespeare, therefore, meant standards of an Arnoldian kind. He was simply and self-evidently 'the best'. Studying Shakespeare would give the elementary school child the necessary moral and cultural uplift; grant him a better life; make him a better citizen. Although Sampson's vision of a society educated by exposure to its own language in its most exalted form might now seem to be the product of a particular historical moment, Newbolt and Sampson between them defined a number of the ground rules by which the question of Shakespeare's place in the nation's education system would continue to be discussed.

First, there was the belief that this most special of authors needed to be taught in special ways. He could not quite be left to speak for himself. The poetical beauties of Shakespeare, the 'word music', might, in swift shafts, be apparent to all, but the language needed mediation, either through the histrionic gifts of the teacher, or through inviting the pupils to participate in the action. Much was required of the teacher.

Second, was the paradoxical belief that despite Shakespeare's unquestionable (and unquestioned) greatness, teaching him was in a way oppositional. To teach him effectively was to draw pupils away from the more numbing experiences of their education and environment: to 'the best' rather than 'the worst'.

Yet, although the Newbolt report is more rewarding as a text than most government reports, it did not lead to any obvious or instant change to the way in which English was taught or studied. Shakespeare maintained a key position in those parts of the curriculum which were examined, and to most school students he would be encountered as part of School Certificate and subsequently GCE English. There were important and isolated practitioners of innovative Shakespeare teaching, such as Caldwell Cook, who in his pioneering use of the 'Mummery' at The Perse School in Cambridge, and in his book *The Play Way* (1917), placed a theatrical approach to Shakespeare at the very centre of his work as an English teacher. Cook died in 1937, but a later pupil at The Perse School, the young Peter Hall, was acutely aware of the legacy:

> My earliest memory of Shakespeare is of a group of eleven-year-olds, armed with wooden shields and swords and cloaks, shouting *Macbeth* at each other . . . The experience of acting the play was immediate and exciting. It never occurred to me not to love Shakespeare. He was thrilling and blood-soaked and full of witches. I wanted to know more about him.[8]

Few pupils in the mid-century were so lucky. Shakespeare was most frequently encountered in the conventional classroom, sitting behind desks, following the text as pupils read it 'round the class'. In *The Disappearing Dais* (1966), a comprehensive and influential guide to English teaching, Frank Whitehead quotes Aldous Huxley:

> Shakespeare did not write his plays to be read, with notes, by children sitting at desks; he wrote them to be acted. Children who have read the plays dramatically, who have lived through them with their whole imaginative being, acquire an understanding of Shakespeare, a feeling for the poetry, denied to those who have ploughed

through them in class and passed, even with honours, an examination in the notes.[9]

Although Whitehead quotes this approvingly, his own attitude to teaching Shakespeare is ultimately more guarded. Whilst he accepts that 'Shakespeare is not only our supreme poet but also our supreme dramatist,' he asks '. . . how many of his plays . . . really come within the linguistic and emotional range of the young adolescent?'.[10]

Whitehead concludes that if pupils 'obviously don't [gain anything from the study of him], we had better cut our losses and abandon Shakespeare in favour of simpler dramatic material. An introduction which doesn't lead to a desire for further acquaintance does no service either to Shakespeare or to the children.'[11] A similar conclusion was reached by J. W. Patrick Creber in *Sense and Sensitivity* (1965), another influential book on English teaching. Creber questions the suitability of Shakespeare for practical drama sessions in school, and believes that he is often introduced to pupils at too early a stage: 'Shakespeare is quite often introduced in the second year [i.e. Year 8], and not only with pupils in selective schools'.[12] This is, of course, precisely the stage at which pupils have been required to study Shakespeare since 1990.

Creber's book, one of the most thoughtful contributions to the history of English teaching in the twentieth century, more explicitly than Whitehead maps out the landscape of 'child-centredness', a landscape much violated by the arrival of the National Curriculum. If Shakespeare has nothing valuable to offer the pupil, then his place in the curriculum is suspect. He can be replaced with something more relevant and engaging, or left until later. Hence the marginalization of Shakespeare for a period in the lower levels of the national examination system. The CSE examination which came into existence in the

1960s did not make Shakespeare compulsory, nor was he so when the two-tier examination system was streamlined into GCSE in 1988.

One of the consequences of Shakespeare's partial and temporary dislocation from the centre of English studies in schools was that those teachers who wished to teach him became in due course able to make use of approaches which had their origin outside the world of education. Jan Kott's *Shakespeare Our Contemporary* (1965) perhaps best symbolizes this trend. Kott's work was a provocative blend of the theatrical and the academic. Although a university professor in Warsaw, a good deal of what Kott had to say about the meaning of Shakespeare for his contemporaries was based on the way in which he had seen Shakespeare interpreted in recent theatrical productions. The English version of his book carried a Preface by the director Peter Brook. Kott's chapter on *Hamlet* perhaps best sums up his approach, specifically where he re-creates the character of Hamlet from two recent performances he had seen in Poland:

> Every Hamlet has a book in his hand . . . Hamlet in the Cracow production . . . read only newspapers. He shouted that 'Denmark's a prison,' and wanted to improve the world. He was a rebellious ideologist . . . Hamlet in the Warsaw production . . . was full of doubts again . . . he was the 'sad boy with a book in his hand' . . . We can easily visualize him in black sweater and blue jeans. The book he is holding is not by Montaigne, but by Sartre, Camus or Kafka. He studied in Paris, or Brussels . . . He returned to Poland three or four years ago. He very much doubts if the world can be reduced to a few simple statements.[13]

Kott's Hamlet wears a 'black sweater and blue jeans', not the doublet and hose of Olivier in the 1948 film. Shakespeare has ceased to be a pageant or a museum piece. He has become transferable to other cultures in a way in which stage productions in the second half of the twentieth century increasingly began to highlight. It was not simply 'Shakespeare in modern dress', but a more powerful perception that Shakespeare could both illuminate and be illuminated by other historical contexts. Hence a fascist *Julius Caesar*, a Crimean *Othello*, a Victorian *Merchant of Venice*, an Edwardian *All's Well that Ends Well*.

The 1960s and 1970s also saw the experimental work of Charles Marowitz, whose 'collage' approach to *Hamlet* and *Macbeth* endeavoured to '[make] contact with that work's essence'.[14] Of his adaptation of *Macbeth,* Marowitz wrote that he had 'tried to locate its metaphysical centre and peel away the pseudo-religious and irrelevantly-political gauzes that had woven themselves around the work'.[15] Those who were hostile to the Shakespeares of Kott or Marowitz could quickly accuse these authors of irreverence. Shakespeare was not being allowed to speak for himself: the timeless voice of the greatest poet was being mutilated in order to make him fit for consumption by those who could not take the trouble to understand him. The fact that Shakespeare had been adapted and amended to suit the varying tastes of audiences since the seventeenth century became easy to forget. The debt of Sue Gregory (in Chapter 2 of this book) to Kott goes beyond her chapter's title. Both she and Elaine Harris (in Chapter 3) acknowledge that if Shakespeare is to be part of the experience of twelve-year-olds in the inner city or the new town, he has to be approached by means of a variety of strategies which will make him answerable to these pupils' understanding of life. This means, amongst other things, accepting that

Shakespeare is as much a star of the big screen, as of the wooden O.

The teaching of Shakespeare has also been influenced by developments within academia. As Tiffany Stern points out in Chapter 6, the teaching of Shakespeare in higher education has been transformed by the critical debates of the 1980s. These have also affected the way in which Shakespeare is taught in schools, particularly to older pupils (see Sean McEvoy's discussion in Chapter 5). The 1980s provided a number of new perspectives on Shakespeare, as both a literary and educational phenomenon. The rather belated arrival of critical theory in Britain caused shockwaves throughout university English departments, as explicitly post-structuralist, Marxist, feminist and – perhaps most significantly for Shakespeare – new historicist and cultural materialist readings of his works were published. A good deal of Shakespeare criticism in the 1980s was not only radical in method, but, politically, explicitly oppositional at a time when the Conservative government was taking a hostile stance towards universities, and by extension, to intellectuals generally.

The titles of some of the critical works published in the 1980s are revealing: *Alternative Shakespeares*, *Political Shakespeare*, *Reinventing Shakespeare*, *That Shakespeherian Rag*, *The Shakespeare Myth*.[16] Bardolatry of the kind that had existed more or less unimpaired since the time of Raleigh was seriously interrogated, and found wanting. The Shakespeare who had been seen as the repository of 'universal truth' was a construct of the educational and political Right, who wished to make him the highest priest of their own elitist culture. His institutionalization by the Royal Shakespeare Company at Stratford, by the National Theatre, by the BBC (who were at the time presenting a complete cycle of the plays on television) and by the reconstructed Globe Theatre was seen as the means by which an ultimately fraudulent representation of Shakespeare as the greatest figure in our literary culture was being upheld. The historicist critics argued that to see Shakespeare's plays outside of other kinds of contemporary discourse was distorting. Research into theatrical and printing house practices showed that there was no such thing as a definitive Shakespearian text. As Alan Sinfield wrote: 'the textual scholar and the theatre enthusiast are arguing in different terms . . . There is no determinate entity called Shakespeare's play . . .'.[17] In an essay specifically about Shakespeare and education, Sinfield went on to attack the assumption, deeply embedded in public examination question papers, 'that Shakespeare is the great National Poet who speaks universal truths'.[18] He was also critical of the way in which, at least at that time, Shakespeare was consciously dehistoricized: 'At no point do the GCE papers of 1983 invite candidates to consider the ways in which a play relates to its social context in Shakespeare's time or subsequently . . .'.[19]

Yet the cause of Shakespeare in schools was, at this time, being advanced precisely by those to whom Sinfield and other academic critics were most deeply opposed. Kenneth Baker, Secretary of State for Education from 1986 to 1989, and architect of the National Curriculum, believed strongly in the 'cultural heritage' model of literary education, and of studying Shakespeare 'in that thorough textual way which meant one really had to know the play backwards'.[20] Baker appointed a committtee, under the chairmanship of Professor Brian Cox, to determine the shape of the National Curriculum English programme. This involved providing lists of suggested reading for pupils at each of the key stages. Shakespeare was the only author to be compulsory, although the Department of Education and Science (DES) document *English for Ages 5–16* (1989) is careful to avoid imposing any particular methodology of teaching:

. . . every pupil should be given at least some experience of the plays or poetry of Shakespeare. Whether this is through the study, viewing or performance of whole plays or of selected poems or scenes should be entirely at the discretion of the teacher.[21]

It is also cautious about the question of Shakespeare's canonical eminence:

Many teachers believe that Shakespeare's work conveys universal values, and that his language expresses rich and subtle meanings beyond that of any other English writer. Other teachers point out that evaluations of Shakespeare have varied from one historical period to the next, and they argue that pupils should be encouraged to think critically about his status in the canon.[22]

Thus – and thus tentatively – was Shakespeare instated as a compulsory part of the educational experience of every child in England and Wales.

After the initial shell-shock, there was something enabling in all this. The DES document had not come clean about which Shakespeare it preferred: iconic, relevant or historical. A book entitled *Shakespeare in the Changing Curriculum* (1991), edited by Lesley Aers and Nigel Wheale, was thus able to address the issues which the new National Curriculum posed. Aers' position was clear:

There is no way that they [school pupils] are going to be sympathetic with tentative claims that Shakespeare offers them a vital human experience . . . Teachers are already working out, very successfully, strategies to show that Shakespeare is 'relevant'.[23]

In a chapter on teaching Shakespeare in schools, Bob Allen teased out the arguments for and against the teaching of Shakespeare. In reply to the question 'What's wrong with teaching Shakespeare?' Allen suggested, first, that the plays were politically suspect, tending to promote right-wing views about such matters as authority and class; second, that setting them as texts for examination purposes encouraged candidates to be 'cautious and deferential'[24]; and third, that teachers and examiners wrenched the plays from their historical context and spent too much time thinking about 'character' ('an unstable and problematic' term).[25]

Going on to consider the question 'Why should we teach Shakespeare?' Allen acknowledged that the very nature of critical debate on Shakespeare made him important, and that he was a significant poet, whom we should teach if we think that poetry matters. He granted Shakespeare considerable insight into the human condition, but also stressed that 'No consistent single ideological position [is] adopted by him'.[26] He also argued that, in order to meet the requirements of all pupils, something other than 'deskbound approaches' needed to be adopted.

Both Aers and Allen, in rejecting deskbound approaches, and acknowledging recent developments in making Shakespeare 'relevant', were nodding in the direction of the significant work that had been done in the 1980s by a number of teachers throughout the country, under the direction of Rex Gibson, for the Leverhulme Trust-funded 'Shakespeare in Schools' project. The breadth and enthusiasm of this project were undeniable. The project issued the major plays for school use in a new set of editions, as well as a number of books and guides designed not only for secondary but also for primary teachers, because, in Gibson's view, it is never too early to start work on Shakespeare. Indeed, one of the consequences of the literacy hour in primary schools is that pupils can now be introduced to Shakespeare as a matter of course at an earlier age than ever before. Gibson is a lover of lists and tables. In *Secondary School Shakespeare: Classroom Practice* (1990), he offers 25 initial recommendations to those planning to teach Shakespeare. It would be superfluous to repeat them here, but it is interesting to note the mixture of reverence and irreverence which informs them. Whilst we are reminded that 'The language has its own unique validity and power',[27] we are also encouraged to 'Play with Shakespeare – he'll survive'[28] and to 'Relax about covering the whole play'.[29] The emphasis is on activity: pairwork, role-play, hot-seating, improvisation – any approach, in fact, which can promote positive engagement with what might otherwise seem daunting and unapproachable material. In its aims, the 'Shakespeare in Schools' project is the logical extension of the 1908 English Association pamphlet and the recommendations of both Newbolt and Cox. The project has been hugely influential, asked a great many fundamental questions about Shakespeare teaching and has encouraged large numbers of teachers to be confidently experimental in their methods. Nevertheless, it is open to the criticism that this is Shakespeare by overkill, that it tries to make Shakespeare not only our contemporary, but all things to all men (and women). As Bob Allen notes, the 'Shakespeare in Schools' approach can cause pupils to '. . . cut and paste the text . . . [and can involve] drama activities [which] can . . . conceal real muddle and lead to a free-for-all in which the potential richness of Shakespeare *as* Shakespeare somehow is missed'.[30] Elaine Harris attests to the stimulus of the project's approach (Chapter 3), whilst also noting where it stops short in an educational culture that is ultimately 'concerned with assessing written responses from critically sensitive, articulate writers' (below, p. 43).

The 1980s was clearly a crucial decade for Shakespeare studies in both school and university. On the one hand there was the belief from the political right that Shakespeare was an intrinsic part of our cultural heritage, and should therefore be studied compulsorily in schools, presumably in the way favoured by Kenneth Baker. On the other, there was the populist work of Rex Gibson's project of trying to make Shakespeare everyone's Shakespeare. Meanwhile, in the universities, the process of historicizing Shakespeare, of removing him from his pedestal as the timeless purveyor of universal truths, was redefining the terms on which senior school pupils and undergraduates would study Shakespeare.

It is easy to be triumphalist about the current situation. In schools, Shakespeare's reputation has been preserved by his incorporation into the National Curriculum. In higher education, as Tiffany Stern points out (Chapter 6), he remains a persistent if transmuted presence in courses for undergraduates. At the same time, it is worth asking exactly who or what has triumphed. Traditional apologists for 'the bard' would suggest that he remains central to the educational experiences of students because he will always be with us. A closer look at the educational culture of recent decades might see more compromise. A criticism of government policy towards the teaching of English has always been that the programmes of study are fixed by the philistines rather than the genuinely informed, and it is a not altogether inaccurate reading of recent educational history to see Shakespeare as having been arbitrarily imposed on the nation's schoolchildren.

One point on which the authors of the following chapters concur is that to teach Shakespeare requires effort. Teaching Shakespeare does not stop at the classroom door. Sue

Gregory's Shakespeare manifests himself on wall-displays in public corridors; the Shakespeares of Joseph Francis and Elaine Harris expand into extra-curricular time; Catherine Alexander's is opened out to students on-site at Stratford-upon-Avon; Tiffany Stern's Shakespeare is not merely the property of the young.

This book is written by professional educators, but it is not a teachers' handbook. It is an attempt to assess the position of Shakespeare in a variety of contrasting educational environments, and to understand how it came to be so. Although inevitably selective, it aims to show where Shakespeare can be found in the educational experience of students of differing ages and in different places.

It would be too grandiose to pronounce that Shakespeare is alive and well in our education system, but it seems perfectly accurate to conclude that he is surviving.

Notes

1. Walter Raleigh, *Shakespeare* (Macmillan, English Men of Letters Series, 1907), p. 2.
2. The English Association, *The Teaching of English in Schools* (Leaflet No. 7, 1908), p. 1.
3. *Ibid.*, p. 2.
4. *Ibid.*, p. 7.
5. *The Teaching of English in England* (HMSO, 1921), pp. 312, 319.
6. *Ibid.*, p. 319.
7. George Sampson, *English for the English* (Ed. Denys Thompson, Cambridge University Press, 1970), p. 113.
8. Peter Hall, *Making an Exhibition of Myself* (Sinclair-Stevenson, 1993), p. 37.
9. Frank Whitehead, *The Disappearing Dais* (Chatto and Windus, 1966), p. 133.

10. *Ibid.*, p. 145.

11. *Ibid.*, p. 146.

12. J. W. Patrick Creber, *Sense and Sensitivity* (University of London Press, 1965), p. 86.

13. Jan Kott, *Shakespeare Our Contemporary* (Methuen, 1967), p. 56.

14. Charles Marowitz, *The Marowitz Shakespeare* (Marion Boyars, 1978), p. 12.

15. *Ibid.*, p. 15.

16. John Drakakis (ed.), *Alternative Shakespeares* (Methuen, 1985); Jonathan Dollimore and Alan Sinfield (eds) *Political Shakespeare* (Manchester University Press, 1985); Gary Taylor, *Reinventing Shakespeare* (Hogarth Press, 1990); Terence Hawkes, *That Shakespeherian Rag* (Methuen, 1986); Graham Holderness (ed.), *The Shakespeare Myth* (Manchester University Press, 1988).

17. *Political Shakespeare*, p. 130.

18. *Ibid.*, p. 138.

19. *Ibid.*, p. 140.

20. Kenneth Baker, *The Turbulent Years* (Faber and Faber, 1993), p. 9.

21. *English For Ages 5–16* (HMSO, 1989) Chapter 7, Paragraph 7.15.

22. *Ibid.*, Paragraph 7.16.

23. Lesley Aers and Nigel Wheale (eds), *Shakespeare in the Changing Curriculum* (Routledge, 1991), p. 35.

24. *Ibid.*, p. 42.

25. *Ibid.*, p. 42.

26. *Ibid.*, p. 45.

27. Rex Gibson, *Secondary School Shakespeare: Classroom Practice* (Cambridge University Institute of Education, 1990), p. 2.

28. *Ibid.*, p. 3.

29. *Ibid.*, p. 6.

30. Lesley Aers and Nigel Wheale (eds), *Shakespeare in the Changing Curriculum* (Routledge, 1990), p. 49.

CHAPTER 2

Making Shakespeare our contemporary: teaching *Romeo and Juliet* at Key Stage Three

Sue Gregory

In the contemporary Baz Luhrmann film version of *Romeo and Juliet*, a sign for petrol creaks in the breeze. On it is written: 'Add more fuel to your fire. PHOENIX.' This is an omen of what is to come when a fire is started over a pool of petrol. It is Tybalt's discarded cigarette that lights it, and a whole stream of the stuff ignites, blazing swiftly until there is a wall of flame, and then a screen of smoke. Tybalt has caused an inferno even though he says he hates the word 'Hell' along with the word 'peace'! With this tower of flame, the description 'the fiery Tybalt' is made visual symbolically on screen. It is the first incident that we witness in the battle between the Montagues and the Capulets, and it is incendiary stuff!

Since September 11 2001 and the burning of the Twin Towers of the World Trade Centre in New York, the opening imagery of the Luhrmann film has even greater impact and relevance. We would wish it were not so, but the young of the world are no longer as innocent as they were prior to that date. All have witnessed living hell, a symbolic annihilation on a vast scale in the name of one fundamentalist ideology's concept of goodness and its bid for heaven. Children and adults alike have had to confront paradoxes as complex as any of those posed by Tybalt. Indeed, the latter suddenly seems to take on a terrorist's mentality, as if Shakespeare could foresee the kind of mind-set which would lead to civil disobedience of the most terrifying kind and leave many of the world's population bewildered, so contradictory and anti-life does it appear.

Of course, many of the world's children have, along with their parents, cheered the attack on America, particularly those who have not been granted an innocence, but have witnessed the slaughter of their fathers as a regular occurrence. And just as children in New York witnessed the horrors of the al-Qaida attack, so children in Afghanistan and Iraq have had their night skies lit with missiles and what security they had pulverized by bombs. There are no winners among the civilian populations of such attacks. As Shakespeare and his prince well knew, 'All are punished.'

More than ever, *Romeo and Juliet* appears to be one vast allegory. The fragile hope of love against the odds. The poverty of the apothecary poisoning that love. As the comparatively affluent West seems increasingly to acknowledge, the war on terrorism must also be a war on world poverty. Yet at least some of the perpetrators of the September 11th massacre were, like Tybalt, from moneyed backgrounds; they were educated men.

Some claim that children learn to cope with a frightening world by experiencing fear through literature, be it between the pages of a Harry Potter novel or in a Baz Luhrmann film of a play by Shakespeare. It seems more necessary than ever that children appreciate from as young an age as possible what happens if two children, two adults, two households, two countries, two religions, two races, two ideologies cannot accommodate each other. The racist backlash in Britain alone after September 11th is likely to have exacerbated many a Romeo and Juliet story. As we study the play, we remind our students that the warring of the Montagues and the Capulets is a civil war; it takes place within a city state. But that does not stop it from being representative of a larger – or a smaller – scenario.

We want our students at high school level to feel that studying *Romeo and Juliet* is relevant, indeed important, to their growing knowledge of the world. To feel that art in all its forms is an expression of what it is to live, that art matters because it helps us to understand our lives a little, and maybe helps us to cope. For these reasons we want our students' experience of studying the play to be as dramatic, as colourful, as imaginative, as intellectully challenging and stimulating as a production of the play. We try to make our visual display based on our study as stunning as we can, so that students cannot avoid being arrested by it as they make their way round the school.

Ours is a high school with ten- to fourteen-year-old students. It is set in a suburb, with many of the children coming from private housing but also a relatively high number who come from outside of the catchment area, from estates in the city of Leicester and from homes in remote villages, so it is a mixed population. It is culturally mixed, too, although with a preponderance of Caucasian children. Students are taught in mixed-ability classes. The school places high value on dramatic presentations and student creativity in music, the visual arts and poetry. The headmistress has specifically said that she does not want concentration on SATs results at the expense of the school's reputation for the use of drama in teaching, the colourful display of children's work and its fostering of the writing of poetry. The English department has been very much encouraged in its approach, and other departments have collaborated with it, in particular the art and science departments.

The English department has worked together on its approach to the study of *Romeo and Juliet*, with leeway for particular teacher enthusiasms. We wanted it to be as broad a study as possible, drawing on other curriculum areas. We wanted it to be accessible to, and pleasurable for, those who struggle academically, at the same time as being demanding for very able students. We wanted it to incorporate study skills and research, as well as literary study. It has evolved over time and necessarily has had to be modified on occasions, but this chapter deals with what I still consider preferred practice, together with its rationale.

Having so many younger students, the more razzamatazz and glamour that we can muster to advertise the play, the more likely we are to generate heightened expectations. It was helpful when *Romeo and Juliet* was one of the set plays for examining at Key Stage Three, when the work achieved was looked up to and viewed as a kind of apprenticeship, a landmark on the way to maturity, as the students moved on to the upper school next door, which takes fourteen- to eighteen-year-olds, where Shakespeare would be studied at Key Stage Four and A-level.

Romeo and Juliet still remains for me the most relevant Shakespeare play to approach with Year 9 students for all the clichéd reasons; the main characters are the same age as them: it is about testing boundaries with authority figures: it contains teenage brawling: the Luhrmann film reflects the street experience of inner city students: it is about the difference between loving and doting: it is about love at first sight, and raises the question of how far this may merely be a matter of two beautiful people desiring one another. Yet it is an idealized love – a love-as-one-might-wish-it-to-be – so that the audience longs for it to succeed against the odds. It is about being obsessed, and it is about two young people with the most high-flown romantic ideals suddenly having it brought home to them that 'life is real, life is earnest'. It carries the deepest possible implications spiritually as well as morally. Yet at a pinch it is a suitable study for Year 8 students as well as Year 9.

Our students will already have some experience of a Shakespeare play from when they were ten-year-olds, when they will have encountered *Macbeth* or, in some cases, *The Tempest*. During that study too there will have been an emphasis on display; collages of good and evil using headlines, pictures and stories from magazines and newspapers. It is an approach that the English department uses when studying and writing poetry, as children can find figurative language difficult and to make imagery concrete helps to make sense of it. With symbols before their eyes, children become more aware of the symbolic associations that words can carry. Display work has led to creative descriptions, poems and literary criticism based on the poetry of (for example) Coleridge, Keats and Blake.

Taught to mixed-ability classes, the Baz Luhrmann version of *Romeo and Juliet* enables students to take from it what they will, according to their intellectual capacity. At one end of the spectrum this may mean the most straightforward grasping of its complex plot and an enjoyment of its excitement, romance and drama, at the other a consideration of the deepest implications of the tragedy. This is where the play becomes terrifying – too frightening, it has to be admitted, for the age group if they are going to take its full impact. Fortunately, there are few students perhaps who think deeply enough about it in their early teens to have their blood run completely cold. Many, however, are likely to feel a sense of pity at the sight of two young people forced by impossible circumstances to do violence to themselves. Few are going to appreciate that evil has comprehensively triumphed over good, that the two young people lying in the vault are sacrificial victims to the hate between their families, that for Shakespeare's audience their very souls are in danger because they have committed self-slaughter. More are going to recognize that the raising of two gold statues in memory of the young lovers is a futile and hollow gesture.

At whatever level it is received, we want somehow to make the study of *Romeo and Juliet* personal to every student – vital, passionate and of our time. We do not want the variety of our students' experience – the excitement, the romance, the agitation, the suspense, the pain and the grief – to be reduced by the way that SATs select two scenes for particular study. We want our students to come to SATs confident that they can read complex meaning into the words before them because the themes and images are marked on their memories through the Luhrmann film, through drama, play-scripts, poetry and prose monologues and the display work they have produced.

When we asked Year 8 students what their expectations of Shakespeare had been before we started on *Romeo and Juliet*, the main answer was that they had feared they might be bored but they had not been; they had found that they had had a better impression of Shakespeare when they had studied *Romeo and Juliet*. They put this down partly to the question of SATs, but partly to the characters in *Macbeth* being 'too old'.

We start our study of the play with the students' own drama. This is because as a department we are committed to drama and to students' own creativity as a means to their motivation. Young people are far more interested in one another than they are in any text. Once they have created their own quarrels and fights, they are more likely to be interested in how Shakespeare – and Baz Luhrmann – develop theirs. We outline the basis of the plot. We then ask students to imagine the pretexts for the 'ancient grudge', and let them loose to work on this. This allows us to conduct an oral assessment.

The scenes are acted out to one another, and the best of them may find an outlet on the school stage, in an assembly for another year group. Younger students are thus given an idea of the quarrelling on which *Romeo and Juliet* is based without having the original plot introduced too early – we want them to come to that afresh. Most children love to entertain others, and children love to be entertained. Interestingly, the instinct of most groups is Shakespeare's instinct in *his* opening quarrel: to make the audience laugh. If when children 'go public' on Shakespeare the result is laughter, this is going to put across the idea that to 'do' Shakespeare is fun. Some children may also take away a subliminal message that will grow on them in time: that Shakespeare is not solemn but profound, and that laughter is part of the profundity. Humour helps the world cope with the unutterable.

Drama scripts are word-processed, so that the students have a sense that they can *make* a play as well as having one thrust upon them! A piece of drama that stays in my mind is a nine o'clock news broadcast featuring a story about the building of a by-pass for Verona. The mayor is clearly being bribed by the Montagues to say that the by-pass should cut through Capulet land. The Montagues, so he claims, are offering a public service by constructing blocks of flats to house the poor, the homeless and the elderly. Mr Capulet declares that his land is green-belt 'like English country gardens', and that the by-pass would pollute a city asset. The mayor speaks out for a spaghetti junction built on Capulet land: 'You know my dogs could produce better milk than his cows'.

It is interesting that most groups choose to make their setting for the 'ancient grudge' contemporary, although we make no such stipulation. It is also interesting how much of the students' work draws on a shared television culture. The quarrel is caused, according to one group, by the fact that the Capulets are nouveau riche and the Montagues 'old money'. The latter is associated in the students' minds with over-religiosity, cricket, old-fashioned puddings, classical music and scrupulous tooth-care: 'May I have a diluted Ribena Toothkind, please? It *is* sugar-free?' New money is associated with the cult of cars, careless driving, heavy metal, 'the boozer' and speed: 'Jus' pass it over 'ere. Or I'll be so low, not even a space-rocket'll do the job.'

As part of their self-assessment, students were asked if they had enjoyed the activity. The response was heartening. One student wrote: 'I LOVED IT! I really enjoy drama and I jump at the chance to make people laugh! I think we work well as a group and together we produce some excellent pieces of drama! We argue a bit, but we enjoy it.' I find it significant that it is their drama work that Year 9 students seem most readily to recall from their Year 6 days. One boy who had been in some trouble during his high school days still had the 'Mad Captain' scripts that he and his group produced when they studied *The Tempest* (they had decided that it was not only the tempest that caused the shipwreck, but problems inside the Captain's head). The boy could still recall his work in detail. What interests me is what work students undertake voluntarily out of school hours. Needless to say, it is what they create themselves – particularly drama sketches – that wins through more than any other.

To make the students further acquainted with the play at the simplest level, we offer lunchtime showings of the *Animated Tales* version. It is part of children's culture to watch cartoons, so this approach to Shakespeare is not alien. Moreover, each short film has something imaginative to offer. For me the strength of the *Romeo and Juliet* version is the way that the adults are shown slipping increasingly out of control, while the regular tolling of the cathedral bell suggests the unstoppable approach of the tragedy. I warn students that it is rather quaint, but will give them a basic idea of the plot, some of the most memorable passages and an introduction to each of the characters with a typical quotation. I also stress that the text is articulated very clearly so that it is the easiest way into familiarity with the language. Because the text alternates with a prose narrative in modern English, this version is a useful way into the play. I do not show it to whole classes who may find it too twee and childish, and be put off before we even start. However, I do monitor the response of students closely once we begin to write about the text and recommend most strongly that those who seem hazy about the plot do watch it, giving lesson time over to this while those who have understood the basic plot continue with other activities which they can pursue for themselves.

In the meantime, as a half-year group, we are into the Luhrmann version. This is so fast-moving and visually crammed that we feel students must be allowed to watch it straight through. The language too, amid all the gun swirling and butt swivelling, is not the easiest to latch onto, so we feel that it is best for the students to make of it what they will rather than breaking off for comment, which might easily mean that they lose the thread. Besides which, whether we teachers love it or loathe it, this contemporary version speaks for itself, not least because it is so powerful visually. The music too relieves and helps to cue in the ear.

The barrier to the students before they start on their study of the play is alarm in the face of the language. How, they ask us, will they ever be able to understand 'old English' with all those 'thee's' and 'thou's'? We encourage them to relax and just let the language come at them, reassuring them that they will take in a lot more than they think they can. We also encourage them from the start to think about the play as a series of contrasts: love/hate, youth/age, sun/moon, light/heavy, chaos/form, sweet/gall, too late/too early, and suggest that they think of

ways in which these pairings and polarities can be related to the
plot – for example, the formality of the introduction of Paris as
a potential wooer of Juliet over and against the chaos of the
fight scenes, or the sweetness of Juliet's kisses contrasted with
the poison Romeo drinks for her sake.

At the end of the screening we ask the students to brain-
storm what scenes they have found most memorable in the
film. These have included not the figure of Christ dominating
the city but the tower blocks of the Montague and Capulet
business empires dominating it; Prince, the chief of police in
his helicopter; Juliet in her wings and Tybalt in his horns; the
very manic Mercutio, cross-dressed and flouncing; Mercutio's
defiant gesture, one arm in the air, wrist limp, as he declares
that he has sustained merely 'a scratch'; the devil-face of
Romeo as he pursues Tybalt in a car chase. In contrast with
such scenes is the glimpsing of one another by the lovers
through the fish tank, a hypnotic, almost surreal section,
dream-like and slow, where one eye of each is seen watching
the other in total fascination. We ask students to divide these
images into 'love' and 'hate'.

At this point we feel ready to make a beginning on our
various ways into a visual display. This is to make the imagery
of the play concrete, to assist understanding and to stimulate
written work. We take an entire wall outside one of the
English department rooms for this, ignoring the conventional
and restricting cork board and using drops of red paper from
ceiling to floor. First, we get the students to make illuminated
letters, based on the medieval manuscripts that we show them,
taking a letter each to spell out 'Romeo and Juliet by William
Shakespeare'. Here we pick up on overtly religious language
and symbols from the Luhrmann film. We encourage the
students to incorporate the contrast between love and hate
into each letter.

For example, we may begin with Tybalt. Wearing devil's horns at the Capulet's fancy-dress ball obviously associates him with the principle of evil. The aggressive grinding out of his cigarette is suggestive of his drive towards annihilation. We take him in a specifically Catholic context since the Church in the person of Friar Lawrence plays such an important part in the play. So students may link Tybalt in his nihilism with the betrayal and crucifixion of Christ. One illuminated letter therefore might incorporate a crown of thorns with vine leaves and grapes, representing the redeeming blood of Christ plus a glass of red wine as a fitting toast for lovers. Another might depict guns intertwined with roses, and another a lamb, a lily and a bloody knife. We do not necessarily expect the students to draw such complicated images; they can be computer-generated, or cut from magazines. Pictures from graphic novels and comics are used, designs for tattoos, transfers, images of war cheek-by-jowl with photographs and advice from *Just Seventeen*: anything which makes our study of the play approximate as closely as possible what the students may have to hand or will impact on their imaginations. We want to make it apparent that the play is still taking place now and not so far from home, that it is played out daily whenever powerful rival gangs in or out of school pick a fight, in the warring in the Middle East, Iraq, Russia and the Congo, in the ideological and religious battle lines drawn between India and Pakistan, in the targeting for atrocities of holiday spots perceived to be the playground of the affluent West – and particularly the young. The consequences are the same: innocent victims caught in the cross-fire, peace-loving citizens at the mercy of the warmongers. I have sometimes given an introduction to the parallels behind *West Side Story*, and offered this as a further option for lunchtime viewing. We also introduce the novel *Across the Barricades* by Joan Lingard, in the hope that one or two may follow the story of Kevin and Sadie, one a Protestant, the other a Catholic from Northern Ireland, through the whole series of novels. Joan Lingard's work has a renewed impact with scenes reminiscent of the early 1970s in Belfast often still before our eyes.

Through our requesting illuminated letters that are specifically of a religious as well as an amorous nature, we prepare students for scenes such as the meeting. The lengthy conceit of Juliet's body as a holy shrine, lips as pilgrims, hands as holy palmers and sins purged is so alien to the students' cultures that anything that draws attention to the profoundly religious foundation of the play is a bonus. By using the language of religion in lay terms for furthering their intimacy, Romeo and Juliet are being outrageous right from the start, but at the same time giving expression to the idea of the body as temple. We stress that although Shakespeare, and Luhrmann, use a specifically Christian (Catholic) context, the story is universal and will appear independently of Shakespeare's play in various guises in other classic literatures and in other languages. The story could have any religion as a backdrop, or indeed be cast in a humanist tradition. For instance, the fate of the Crown Prince of Nepal, a Hindu, provides a chilling real-life example from the past. Marriage to a young woman from a royal background, but one that his parents did not consider as 'high' as his own, was denied to him. He turned on himself, but not before he had killed many members of his own royal family. Again the parallel, although by no means exact, is still all too reminiscent of the play.

The Crown Prince of Nepal met his love at a party given by his guardian in a great country house. At this point it seems appropriate to mention the soliloquies that the students write based on the meeting or the balcony scene. We ask students to write a soliloquy because many can draw on their own infatuations. It also affords students the opportunity to give expression to love as well as hate. Moreover, it allows them to experiment with a different kind of writing and makes them more aware of how Shakespeare solved the problem of conveying a character's thoughts to his audience. We also want students to recognize the suggestion of the rich inner life that makes a Shakespearian hero or heroine so memorable. We do not limit the boys to writing as Romeo or the girls as Juliet. Sources for the students have included love lyrics and love poems, extracts from *The Song of Solomon* and the *Faber Book of Seductions* (something one girl brought in for herself). A number achieved genuinely heightened language, illustrating the emotion of their soliloquies with art postcards, for example reproductions of the work of Gustav Klimt.

From the beginning, we have the text available for those who want to read either the entire play or parts of it in detail. We have enough copies available for each member of a half-year to have one, and have three different editions, the most popular of which is the Stanley Thornes, which has a modern version of the text next to the original. We also have academic dictionaries to hand (the double Oxford dictionary) so that students can look up what challenging words in the text meant in Shakespeare's day. Some able students in the past have chosen to examine in detail the many paradoxes Romeo uses when speaking of the feud and of Rosaline, as a way of furthering their study of opposites. Others have chosen to look closely at the Prince's speech from Act One to examine the problems that he is encountering. This has been particularly relevant given the problems the police have faced in Bradford, Oldham and so on. Students are asked to investigate quotations and individual words: for example, we encourage them to consider the double meaning of 'Throw thy mis-temper'd weapons to the ground' (I provide material on the tempering of steel, reminding students that swords are most commonly

used in productions and not guns). Students who are capable
of working like this have a real interest in language and we use
demanding vocabulary when discussing their study with them,
incorporating a wide range of precise and abstract words
(archetype, soul, perpetrator, ambiguous, paradoxical, irony,
civil, malevolent, benevolent), explaining ourselves as the need
arises.

A way forward for the future would be to tackle the set
scenes in this way, working with mixed-ability groups and
leaving it up to them, with prompting, to tease out the
meaning, coming together at the end to work through the
whole scene together. The only reason I have not attempted
this in the past is the fear that there would be a loss of focus if
the students found it too difficult a task. Also, if we work
through the set scene as a class, everybody gets to hear the
more inspired of student comments.

I encourage students to research the background of the play.
Did Italy exist as such in the sixteenth century? What wars
would Shakespeare have experienced or heard about? Find out
the original moral that lay behind the source story of *Romeo
and Juliet* and see what Shakespeare did with it. We want them
to speculate. What kind of man do they consider Shakespeare
might have been, both from the knowledge on the plot and
from the very different moral spin that he gave to his source
material? In what century do they imagine *Romeo and Juliet*
took place in Shakespeare's imagination? We want students to
undertake such tasks so some will appreciate that all art comes
out of a specific cultural and political context, but that artists
are free to make what they will of this.

Those who would balk at a broader study of the play are
allowed to conserve their intense concentration for the set
scenes. This is only fair in a mixed-ability class. We want
everybody to know the whole play by seeing the film, but

sustained reading is not for all. Concentrating on set scenes means that everybody experiences the original language (even if some need support in reading it), to which they can bring a broader knowledge of plot, character and themes. Extensive use is made of the library and of the Internet. Students are expected to work on their own, in pairs and in small groups, and my expectations are high. I want the tasks to be appropriately demanding and involving, and to promote knowledge and comprehension. I also want them to contribute to classroom thoughtfulness.

In addition to the books already mentioned, I provide as wide a range of resources as possible: art postcards, art books, reference books and articles, travel books. Many students bring in resources of their own. I want to encourage an analytical response – analysing language and character, sharply focusing on evidence – and I want much discussion to arise out of research. I allow students to take off imaginatively in their choice of research topic from the Luhrmann film or from fringe interests in Shakespeare's text. For some, the apothecary's shop provides a rewarding line of study – the kinds of poisons that would have been available in the sixteenth century and earlier, and what remedies Friar Lawrence, as herbalist, might concoct. What were/are the nearest equivalent to the knock-out drops that Friar Lawrence prescribes for Juliet? What is meant by 'on pain of torture', and what kind of tortures were around in the sixteenth century and earlier? Torture suggests Hell, and Shakespeare's audience would have believed in Hell. How did they imagine it? (Pictures are available.) Students might like to investigate astrology and its history, since Romeo speaks of 'Some consequence, yet hanging in the stars.' Others may become interested in riot gear, and collect stories from newspapers, television and radio about the warring factions in the world's cities. Students look for Verona on a map, photocopy it, encircle it and look for the town in travel catalogues. Those who read in detail are quick to point out the romantic claim that the stone of Verona's old buildings is pinkish in colour.

I include religious images such as those depicting the Last Supper, so that students take on board the idea of the sacrificial meal and the spiritual significance of eating together. We talk about the shared food associated with festivals across different religions. This we contrast with the secular feast of the Capulets, provided as an exotic backdrop for the introduction of Paris to the daughter of the house, an alliance embarked upon with the worldliest of motives. Crucifixions bring home the idea of innocence being sacrificed to cleanse the world of sin. We talk about Romeo and Juliet as sacrificial lambs, engaged by default in self-slaughter as a result of their parents' hate.

I provide art books depicting war for those who are interested, since it is war that wins in *Romeo and Juliet*, and we can depend on the students to bring in their own images of love and beautiful people! I can offer images by Goya and Picasso (*Guernica* and *Korea*), Kathe Kollwitz's drawings, Stanley Spencer's paintings of the First World War, Henry Moore's drawings of civilians sleeping in the London underground during the Second World War. I give historical background to this if requested. By this, I want to encourage discussion – a painting like *Korea* is very accessible, portraying the vulnerability of the civilian in the face of man-as-machine; *Guernica* is much more subtle, and students argue about the point of the bull, the naked light bulb, the baby hanging like a rag-doll. We talk about the part played by children in the Luhrmann film, also the experience of the children in the Holy Cross Primary School and Protestant children who have been taken to school in north Belfast in armoured vehicles.

I want students to appreciate how pictorial art as well as dramatic art stresses the dignity of human life even at its apparently most undignified; how artists draw on the past as Shakespeare and Luhrmann do; how Moore, aware of Dante, seems to make the underground go on eternally, like the mouth of Hell; how Stanley Spencer turns the everyday experience of a soldier into a almost religious image, as Shakespeare does with *Romeo and Juliet*. The pilgrim/holy shrine conceit literally suggests the finger-touch of the everyday with the sublime.

I give groups of students art postcards of portraits so that they can select for the display their own idea of what the characters might have looked like, discussing their impressions of character from the text. For the most able students, this activity is linked to a discussion of responsibility for the tragedy. We also display postcards of Italian towns and cities, so that students see authentic architecture.

In the meantime, for homework, I expect students to keep scrapbooks of their personal response to *Romeo and Juliet*. This might include their play-scripts, love or war poems inspired by the play or that the students particularly like, the write-ups of their research, appropriate newspaper headlines (either their own or cut from papers), their own newspaper accounts, scripts for *News at Ten* (we point out how cleverly the Luhrmann version uses the prologue and epilogue as newscasts), Rosaline's/Juliet's diary, letters, songs, prayers, soliloquies inspired by love, recipes for poison or their own version of Romeo's love poetry (since he is portrayed, aptly, as a love poet in the Luhrmann version).

I also offer a showing of the Zeffirelli version over lunchtime. This is in order for students to be aware of directors as creative artists, with their own interpretations of how the text should be played. Seeing alternative versions also makes students aware of audience, appropriateness and commercial constraint. The bedroom scene is excellent for demonstrating this, with the Zeffirelli film quite explicit at one end of the spectrum, and the *Animated Tales* (which might be shown to primary school children) at the other (in this a flight of twittering birds represents the union of the lovers). Most of the students do watch the Zeffirelli version. Comments have ranged from 'I prefer it to the Luhrmann. It was more realistic and it captured the spirit of the time' (a boy), to 'Not bad. It stuck to the script' (a girl). Obviously, if we can see a live version of the play and have yet a different line on it, this is a bonus. We have had performances visit us in school whenever these have been on offer, including one set in India.

It is hoped that from using the play as a basis for such study our students can learn to be rich and flexible in their capacity to draw allusions and cross-references between cultures, between different times in history and even between different areas of the curriculum. We also want our study to be part of their multicultural, spiritual and moral education. For those who are already film buffs, I mention that Luhrmann is drawing on a rich cinematic tradition, how his *Romeo + Juliet* reminded me in snatches of *Satyricon*, for example, and *Tommy*.

We endeavour to make our broad *Romeo and Juliet* study personal to each student by giving them as wide a choice of approach as possible. The educational danger is that they will become muddled, and that nothing will be studied in depth. But I have not found this. In the end we settle down to careful and detailed exploration of the set scenes as a class. On the way, students have had the chance to run their eye over an abundance of images and to make them their own. They have had plenty of opportunity to respond creatively in whatever way they like to the play, but with the proviso that they provide two base-line assignments, a play-script and a soliloquy, as well as the essays that will arise out of close study of the set scenes. These are each assessed formally as instances of different kinds of writing.

The purpose and aims of this Shakespeare work are communicated on paper to the students so that they can ultimately conduct a self-assessment. The primary purpose of our approach to the study of *Romeo and Juliet* is to present it as relevant to our time. We want students to consider how far they found the Luhrmann film understandable and enjoyable. We also want them to think about how far and in what ways their producing of their own drama, soliloquies, research, display and scrapbooks helped them in this process.

Our aims are to promote much discussion, and to encourage wide reading and different kinds of writing. We ask students to think about how far they took part in discussion – of their own drama, of the video, of images of war, of their research, of the characters and their respective responsibility for the tragedy, of the set scenes. We also want them to think about how much they have read – of the play, of love and war poetry, of newspaper accounts, for research, of relevant fiction, even of the art and literary criticism which I also provide. We want them to consider whether studying the play has made them more aware when watching or listening to the news. Finally, we want students to consider the different kinds of writing they have undertaken: who they perceived their readership to be, what study skills and sources they have used for their research and what of their work they particularly value.

What I tend to find is that the students come to the set scenes relatively fresh. Yet they still seem well capable of fitting them into the context of the rest of the play. They also seem alert to the contrasts within their scenes, and to the switches in mood and temperature. During our last inspection, the English department was praised for encouraging an unusual amount of cross-curricular education, and I believe that it was our approach to *Romeo and Juliet* that partly prompted this.

I like to think that the study of Shakespeare is alive and well. The not-too-demanding and flexible requirements of Key Stage Three allow a degree of freedom to a mixed-ability arrangement. At the same time, the SATs themselves have high expectations, and afford a rigorous academic and empathic study for those who are capable of it. It is a bonus only to have to study two set scenes in depth rather than read the whole play, as we had to do when I was fourteen. It means that we can concentrate on performance rather than text, yet still have the intellectual satisfaction of teasing out meaning and appreciating depth of allusion.

My only fear is that English teaching will become more prescriptive as high school English is squeezed by expectations of a 'literacy hour' approach, and that there will not be time for the more free-wheeling 'scrapbook' method which often leads to both some of the most original creative work of the year and some very interesting research. The scrapbook is most revealing of the calibre and dedication of students, and allows each to make of it what they will. It also means that teacher suggestions of a more individual nature can be forthcoming. It may be impossible to 'assess' formally, since everybody is pursuing different lines. But we all know what Shakespeare had to say about comparisons, in spite of the current emphasis on test results: that they are 'odorous'. In other words, they stink!

CHAPTER 3

New town Shakespeare: a comprehensive school approach at Key Stages Three and Four

Elaine Harris

A teacher of Shakespeare will often begin a programme of lessons by focusing on the common ground between the pupils and the text. From there, it may be possible to move the pupils through the text to a point where they recognize the plays as superbly-written drama and as an important element of their own consciousness. This may be a formidable accomplishment for any English teacher, but it is particularly so in Harlow New Town, where reading Shakespeare often seems such an irrelevant, rarefied, cultural experience.

Finding a point of engagement is considerably more difficult for a teacher in a situation where Shakespeare seems so significantly removed from the students' experiences. My pupils do not have all the advantages of a middle-class upbringing focused on long-term goals, in an atmosphere where education is seen as both extrinsically and intrinsically valuable. A few have learnt English as a second language. Most do not come from homes filled with books or where reading is an activity to be enjoyed during leisure time. Most have never been to a concert or visited an art gallery or attended a live production of a play, apart from the local Christmas pantomime. Most do not have their own computers and most are not living with both parents or relating to adults who have experienced full-time education beyond the age of sixteen. For these pupils, encountering Shakespeare may not be an exciting venture of enrichment providing a uniquely enjoyable educational experience but yet another difficult hurdle in the process towards a respectable level at Key Stage Three or the coveted 'C' pass at GCSE. Some are openly dismissive or antagonistic towards Shakespeare, and those who cooperate often do so at the outset, with a wearied spirit of forbearance. In demographic terms, my pupils come from homes where incomes are low and divorce rates are high. Accordingly, they lack the stability and vision of the middle classes. Low self-image and a poor cultural background ensure that they rarely aspire to university places.

Nevertheless, much is expected of English teachers who are required, even at Key Stage Three level, to educate pupils to a fairly advanced standard. In the wider spectrum of Shakespeare studies, the richness and complexity of learning continues through school and university to doctorate level. But with limited time and resources, teachers at lower secondary level must prepare pupils for a written examination that will require them to grasp the dramatic impact of particular scenes, show understanding of the way Shakespearian characters function and demonstrate critical sensitivity towards the language. The difficulty of this must not be underestimated. Battling with challenging texts, and reluctant or even obstructive pupils, such teachers are inevitably forced to condense, 'cut corners' or seek the most appealing lesson plans. Since they are also concerned with their own survival in the classroom, they may show films of the play and use only a few selected passages as the basis for a broad understanding of the plot. At worst, preparation for the examination may consist of a few lively dramatic presentations, some discussion exploring general issues and some rudimentary comprehension.

Consequently, many children are often inadequately prepared. Whereas nearly all are encouraged to experience a sense of dramatic involvement, writing fluently, authoritatively and coherently about the plays – the very skills on which they will be judged – the plays themselves are undervalued or given insufficient attention. Indeed, the type of critical appreciation that involves a close study of the language may be confined to a few lessons and, where streaming exists, the more able will usually be given considerably more opportunity to practise the necessary academic skills. In most comprehensive schools, there is the need for a clearer balance between active participation and sufficient practice in the more exacting discipline of literary appreciation.

Teachers, inspired by Shakespeare's plays, usually recognize that while the language is a barrier to an initial understanding, the plays work as narratives and offer considerable scope for dramatic involvement. For these reasons and because they are concerned with engendering a positive response, they are tempted and, perhaps, even advised, to follow Rex Gibson's approach. The undeniable recent success of the 'Shakespeare in Schools' project and the proliferation of literature it has encouraged, has provided several teachers with points of entry and ready-made schemes of work relating to most of the Shakespeare canon. It is an energetic approach, releasing pupils from their traditional position behind desks and engaging them in tasks as 'active' learners. Pupils often begin to enjoy the activity of play-acting, immersing themselves in character, grasping the dramatic possibilities of particular scenes and experimenting with a variety of readings of specific speeches. Gibson expounds his ideas clearly in *Teaching Shakespeare*, a title designed as a handbook for teachers:

The commitment of this book is to active methods of teaching Shakespeare. Shakespeare was essentially a man of the theatre who intended his words to be spoken and acted out on the stage. It is in the context of dramatic realism that the plays are most appropriately understood and experienced. The consequence for teaching is clear: treat the plays as plays for imaginative enactment in all kinds of different ways.[1]

Surely excellent advice for encouraging involvement and participation but, while relishing this freedom, teachers know that although Shakespeare intended his words to be spoken, the examining bodies of the National Curriculum, at both key stages, are concerned with assessing written responses from critically-sensitive, articulate writers. The plays are more than just the means to a dramatic presentation. Indeed, the language must be valued for its poetic as well as its dramatic power. Pupils who appreciate this will have a depth of engagement that, while enabling them to achieve good results in the short term, may broaden their capacity for appreciating literature and ultimately influence their understanding of the world.

It is important to recognize the difficulty of comprehending Shakespeare's language at all stages of the teaching process, but for several pupils, this is the barrier to their engagement with the text on a literal level, even before they can begin to appreciate its poetry. Enthusiastic, well-meaning drama teachers may try too hard to minimize this difficulty. Margareta de Grazia reminds us that 'we tend to overlook the fact that four centuries separate Shakespeare's English from our own'[2], while Frank Kermode makes an even stronger case for seeing the language as central and of being challenging for both modern and Elizabethan adult audiences:

The life of the plays is in the language. Yet the language can admittedly be difficult, even baffling. This is obviously so for audiences coming in four hundred years after the event, but it must have been true also of the original audiences, less because the language itself was unfamiliar (though much more so to us) than because of the strange and original uses an individual writer might put it to. It is true that the audience, many of them oral rather than literate, were trained, as we are not, to listen to long, structured discourses, and must have been rather good at it, with better memories and more patience than we can boast.[3]

Such views may help teachers to respect the complaints of pupils who fail to understand or find deciphering the language a dark, cheerless struggle rather than an illuminating experience. As with learning to play the piano, the rewards do not come instantly because the task of becoming familiar with the unfamiliar requires application and patience. Moreover, at Key Stage Three, pupils are usually embarking on such material for the first time. A skilful teacher involved in tackling a Shakespeare text must focus on the language and, perhaps, through a judicious selection of passages encourage both understanding and appreciation. In his opening paragraph to *Shakespeare's Language*, Kermode claims contentiously that 'Shakespeare is studied almost to death, but the fact that he was a poet has somehow dropped out of consideration'.[4] Pupils must be educated to encounter Shakespeare, the poet as well as Shakespeare, the dramatist. Michael Dobson's question is surely relevant here: 'Which conventional phrase best describes the author of *Hamlet*, "the world's greatest poet" or "the world's greatest playwright"?'[5]

My concern is with enabling pupils to approach Shakespearian language with a sense of dramatic and personal involvement. They should, as Gibson recommends, see 'the plays as plays', but they should also have the confidence to write knowledgeably and eloquently, grasping a play's richness and potential for aesthetic power as well as its dramatic or narrative impact. Drama, although popular and valuable in teaching Shakespeare, is a means to an end, not an end in itself. At both key stages, teachers are concerned with the development of their pupils' critical sensibilities towards the language as well as with the appeal of the lessons.

Teaching *Macbeth* at Key Stage Three

Having accepted both the difficulty of understanding the language and the necessity for doing so, teachers would be well-advised to clarify their aims when setting out to teach Shakespeare. In the English department of my Harlow school, the following objectives are thought to be important:

- approaching the plays with confidence and enjoyment;
- having a sense of ownership of the play;
- being involved in active learning rather than passive reception;
- understanding the basic plot;
- responding to characters by showing an interest in their development, relationships and roles within the play;
- writing articulately and fluently about the play – showing a sense of structure and critical engagement;
- exploring the language – showing the ability to appreciate and criticize significant images and rhythmic and metrical effects.

Examiners assume that teachers select the texts to be studied at Key Stage Three. In my school, we have challenged this assumption by frequently providing the pupils with a choice. At Key Stage Three this would necessarily be limited to three texts, but where the year group is 'blocked' (i.e. taught at the same time) there is scope for an ambitious coherent department to experiment with alternative ways of grouping and selecting the plays. Teachers' personal preferences regarding particular texts must be considered important. With the help of colleagues, teachers of Key Stage Three are asked to direct and enact small scenes that encapsulate some of the major concerns of their preferred texts. Pupils then watch scenes from all three texts and select the play that appeals to them. Even if they fail to understand some of the language at this stage, there is a marked difference between the atmospheres of *Macbeth, Henry V* and *Twelfth Night* (the texts for Key Stage Three at the time of writing).

Accordingly, the whole venture of teaching Shakespeare begins with a huge theatrical event as a year group or half-year group watches two or three dramatic presentations. In practice, this is a positive way to begin. Teachers are stimulated by the prospect of performing and pupils appreciate that something different and important is happening in English lessons. When they choose their particular text for closer study, they are noticeably more motivated in their approach and attitude. Psychologically, it puts both teachers and learners into a stronger starting position. Furthermore, where the year group is large, there will be opportunities for English staff to create two or three groups committed to the same text. These may be organized according to ability or socially engineered to provide the best results, with special needs assistants deployed where they are most effective.

Once the decisions have been made and the classes formed,

teachers may wish to devote a few initial lessons to the historical background of Shakespeare's theatre. This was recently achieved very effectively by a colleague who recognized the potential of the 'Horrible Histories' satirical popular history series of paperbacks that includes *The Terrible Tudors.*[6] Instead of embarking on a lengthy programme of library research or pointless Internet downloading, she asked her Year 9 class to select and present ten facts connected with Shakespeare's success as a dramatist in the Elizabethan era. They were encouraged to read widely but to present their ideas in the style of *The Terrible Tudors*. Inevitably, the parodying of such an outrageously flippant style in semi-pictorial form led to some entertaining presentations in both oral and written form. One small group seized the opportunity to present their carefully formulated views to the class on an overhead projector. The debate that followed revealed the whole form's depth of background knowledge, growing confidence and sense of fun.

Most teachers beginning work on *Macbeth* welcome the first scene. It is rhythmic, atmospheric and beautifully short, providing clear opportunities for drama, dance, sound effects and most importantly the rhythmic manipulation of language by powerful if 'imperfect speakers' (1.3.70). Kermode points out that these opening lines are a new departure in Shakespeare in that they tell us nothing directly about the subject of the play. The sisters speak in paradoxes: 'false antithesis, ghostly choices, an ironic parody of the human powers of prediction . . . The paradox is oracular; oracles are traditionally equivocal.'[7] A teacher can begin to tackle the language almost immediately by highlighting the lexical echoes in the text. Duncan's pronouncement at the end of the second scene, 'What he hath lost, noble Macbeth hath won' (1.2.69), echoes the 'lost and won' (1.1.4) of the sisters. Similarly, Macbeth's first line, 'So foul and fair a day I have not seen' (1.3.38), obliquely reproduces the witches' paradox that 'Fair is foul, and foul is fair' (1.1.11). By encouraging awareness of such patterns in the language, with or without the relevant literary terms, the teacher will begin to reveal the rich linguistic texture of the play and help to stimulate a curiosity for further examples.

It is probably best at Key Stage Three to concentrate on a unifying theme and then to divide the play into manageable sections. At this level, an obvious but fundamental theme would be the tragic hero's moral descent from his reputation at the beginning, expressed in Duncan's 'Valiant cousin! Worthy gentleman!', to Malcolm's despised 'dead butcher' of the fifth act. One useful division is to focus initially on Acts I and II as a complete narrative section. Most pupils wishing to become involved in the intricacies of the language need to have a firm grasp of the series of events leading to Duncan's death. One way of achieving this quickly is to show part of the popular cartoon version, but another is for the teacher to have placards of the characters' names and to recount the story, while calling upon some pupils to represent particular characters. Using students as chess pieces that can be moved around makes for an interesting narrative discourse. The pupils representing the characters and those in the audience will often ask pertinent questions in order to establish or reinforce their understanding. Under these circumstances, it is a short leap to a discussion of character and motive.

Once the broad brushstrokes of the framework are in place, the pupils are ready to study the play in more detail. For newcomers to Shakespeare's language Scene II, where the bloody captain reports on the battle, often comes as a shock after Scene I. The teacher, needing to maintain momentum, could productively 'edit' the scene, concentrating on particular lines and asking questions that reveal important aspects of the play, such as the violence of the imagery. Most adolescents are fascinated by these violent images. Any belief that *Macbeth* or studying Shakespeare is for 'wimps' or 'boffins' is hastily dispelled. It is important to have the text available in a form on which pupils can mark and mine the lines, perhaps with a selection of fluorescent highlighter pens. So, for example, the class could be asked to highlight the terms that are applied to Macbeth in order to appreciate the high esteem he accrues as a soldier. In another colour, they could be asked to highlight and explain some of the images of violence. Later, these could be compared with the images of violence surrounding the murder of Duncan. As Alan Sinfield points out:

> It is often said that *Macbeth* is about 'evil', but we might draw a more careful distinction: between the violence the state considers legitimate and that which it does not. Macbeth, we may agree, is a dreadful murderer when he kills Duncan. But when he kills Macdonwald – 'a rebel' (1.2.10) – he has Duncan's approval . . .
>
>   . . . Violence is good, in this view, when it is in the service of the prevailing dispositions of power; when it disrupts them, it is evil.[8]

Lady Macbeth's preoccupation with cruelty extends the violence inherent in the play and fulfils the witches' observation that 'Fair is foul and foul is fair'. Her duplicity, powerful rhetoric and 'undaunted mettle' ensure her continuing fascination as a character, and an important question, constantly reiterated by examiners, relates to her role in Macbeth's corruption or moral descent. Although the frisson of her scenes with Macbeth is best explored dramatically, much can be gained from a meticulous examination of the images she evokes and of the manipulative power of her exchanges with Macbeth. The interplay of their speeches begins the moment they meet on stage, making for an exciting pace of delivery:

> **Macb.**   My dearest love,
> Duncan comes here to-night.
> **Lady M.**   And when goes hence?
> **Macb.** Tomorrow, as he purposes.
> **Lady M.**   O! never
> Shall sun that morrow see!
>
> (1.5.57–61)

No teacher should miss the opportunity to emphasize the tension of this scene by encouraging some spirited reading or dramatic presentation, but further appreciation can be encouraged by examining the lines on the page and noting the way in which Lady Macbeth completes Macbeth's metrical lines. George T. Wright makes this point very clearly with a further superb example:

> For one character to complete another's blank verse line is a dramatic as well as a metrical obligation. It also seems normal, though some instances are extreme. Tense after the murder of Duncan, the Macbeths speak four times in one line:
>
> > Did you not speak?
> > When?
> > Now.
> > As I descended? (2.2.16)[9]

The urgent simplicity of this short scene makes it accessible to most pupils: they can easily stage a version in pairs. Simple,

too, is the patterning of the words in this sliding scale, suggestive of both staircases and moral decline.

After Duncan's murder, it is usually necessary to review the
action so far. In my experience, most pupils benefit from
revising some significant points of the narrative before tackling
the next part of the play. The teacher needs, for example, to
elucidate:

- What exactly Macbeth does in the first two acts, i.e. how
  many people does he kill?
- What Lady Macbeth does, i.e. the extent of her practical
  contribution to the murder and her attempts to conceal
  their guilt.
- How Macbeth feels before and directly after the murder.
- Lady Macbeth's reaction to Macbeth's fears.

There are several similar questions that might require the
pupils to re-examine the text in detail. An experienced teacher
would ensure that they are raised in a lively, entertaining way.
One approach could be to ask the pupils to research these
questions for homework and then to use a quiz show structure
to establish that the homework has been completed: *The
Weakest Link*, *Blockbusters* and *University Challenge* can all
be used to good effect.

Macbeth's moral decline accelerates during the next narrative section, which covers Macbeth's employment of the
assassins, Banquo's murder and his subsequent appearance at
the feast. To clarify the sequence of events, the teacher could
stage a mime involving the whole class. Initially, the Shakespearian language and the problems it poses for young
students could be removed in favour of a huge processional
scene that focuses on Macbeth's public role as king. Like the
producer of the film *Barry Lyndon*, I have used the stately

rhythm of Handel's 'Sarabande' to establish the solemnity of the occasion. Against the insistent beat of the funereal music, with pupils arranged formally at a long table, I recount the events, spotlighting particular scenes: Macbeth's conspiracy with the assassins, the murder of Banquo with Fleance's escape, the assassins' reporting to Macbeth, his determination to mingle with the guests, the ghost's appearance, Macbeth's terror and Lady Macbeth's desperate attempts to maintain the social equilibrium. Once the pupils have grasped this dramatic structure, they can begin to appreciate more keenly the language expressing the awful power of Macbeth's imaginings and the recurring key-note of the blood imagery.

Another approach that works well with my pupils is to attempt to externalize what can be appreciated internally or aesthetically. As an example of this, a colleague in my department represented the concept of dramatic tension in graphic terms, measuring its intensity in the quantifiable units of a histogram. Using this visual device on a whiteboard, she chaired a class discussion that began with an exploration of the nature of dramatic tension. This led to an explanation of dramatic irony and a lively debate on the first 'reading' of the dramatic tension temperature gauge as the banquet scene begins. A fruitful disagreement ensued. Some pupils thought that the scene had a relatively calm and welcoming opening in which Macbeth exercised his sociability as a genial host: 'Ourself will mingle with society/ And play the humble host.' Others insisted that, as the audience knows of Macbeth's implication in the murder of Banquo, the atmosphere is already predicated on a sense of unease. Accordingly, his hospitable words disguise his guilt and nervous anticipation of the arrival of the murderers.

Pupils at Key Stage Three will often need and appreciate visual reinforcement of the language. Illustrations of the images in pictorial or diagrammatic form assist in comprehension, making students more confident in handling the text and consequently leading to a greater reliance on their own judgement.

Another colleague in the department had considerable success with shoeboxes. In an attempt to highlight the narrative and significant points of the final part of the play, she took the final scenes and gave each one to a pair of pupils within the class. Each pair was then given a shoebox and asked to construct within it a key moment in their particular scene. The shoebox was used as the stage beyond a proscenium arch. It was lined with sugar paper of an appropriate background, cardboard characters were placed inside and speech bubbles were used for quotations. On the back, the pupils were asked to explain their choice of quotation and dramatic moment. Once all the shoeboxes were complete, the teacher could place them chronologically and represent the final scenes as an impressive series of tableaux. In practice, pupils felt a personal interest in the success of this display. Not only was the dramatic experience of the play made 'concrete' and visual, but pupils spoke fluently about their scenes, reflecting an ownership of the text that is essential to their self-confidence. Selecting quotations and explaining key moments, evaluating the relative importance of their ideas while making links with other parts of the play are the necessary skills that need to inform their writing.

All 'concrete' approaches must, however, inform abstract thought, and teachers must not lose sight of the importance of writing. The Key Stage Three examination in its present form favours writers over readers or performers. With their relative cultural poverty and lack of home support, my pupils are clearly at a disadvantage. School, therefore, must inspire both the motivation and the necessary response to do well in public examinations. In my department, we may make extensive use of some eccentric ideas to enable pupils to experience the full power of the text but, ultimately, we need them to write essays. Oral discussion, dramatic involvement, cutting, sticking and constructing models must all work towards presenting ideas articulately on paper. The frequency of practice where writing is concerned cannot be ignored.

In the final weeks of last year's preparation, we turned to the Internet in order to enlarge our understanding and reading about the play. Downloading a series of useful websites seemed to hold more interest than re-reading the play or skim-reading books of criticism for alternative views. Through a careful choice of websites, pupils were presented with contradictory views and asked to consider and contest them. Where possible they were required to word-process essays and written responses. This exposure to writing, delineating the themes and commenting upon the characters, enabled the pupils to hone their work towards the high standards demanded. They could access a wealth of ideas, quote from the text, learn to identify literary techniques and use the appropriate vocabulary that would develop their skills as budding literary critics. Furthermore, once the teacher had corrected and commented, it was much easier to change or re-work word-processed material. In this way, they were able to develop as writers, taking pride in their achievement.

Thus, *Macbeth*, a play that initially held such terrors for them, was gradually subsumed into their consciousness as a familiar work about which they had views and could articulately and critically explore in writing, even under timed conditions. Screwing their courage 'to the sticking place' and with a belief in success rather than failure, the pupils of my school were able to approach the Key Stage Three National Curriculum Tests with confidence.

Teaching *Much Ado About Nothing* at Key Stage Four

Although teaching Shakespeare at Key Stage Four must meet the specific requirements of a GCSE syllabus, teachers have much more freedom to exercise choice where both the text and the outcomes are concerned. Unlike the straitjacket of the Key Stage Three examination focusing on one of three plays and leading inexorably to a written test, the NEAB syllabus at Key Stage Four gives the teacher the opportunity to range across the Shakespearian canon. Unhampered by a common test and loosely bound by the more flexible criteria of coursework objectives, the teacher is more likely to be influenced by personal inspiration or guided by discretion in selecting a play that reflects the tastes and preoccupations of a particular class.

Harlow teachers welcome this autonomy but learn, through experience, to develop a necessary cunning. Even at Key Stage Four, Shakespeare poses enormous challenges to the comprehension of most Harlow pupils who, at the outset, are only too eager to reject the text as irrelevant or question the point of tackling the original language in written form if a filmed version is available. Although they are ultimately capable of lively response and fresh analytical writing, they need learning experiences designed to encourage a familiarity with the play in order to build the confidence with which to write.

Teachers at Key Stage Four have the scope to provide useful experiences in drama and discussion but, since they are ultimately required to meet examination criteria, they need to ensure that specific outcomes are gained from devoting a whole term to 'Shakespeare'. Consequently, every GCSE candidate in my department is expected to produce three pieces of coursework from a 'Shakespeare Term': a media assignment, an oral exercise and an essay that fulfils the criteria of both English Language and English Literature.

Much Ado About Nothing has proved to be a successful

text at Key Stage Four level within the context of the NEAB syllabus. It has much to offer a group of young people in its preoccupation with the vagaries of love and fashion, and in the irresistible humour of the practical jokes. As the prose style accounts for 72 per cent of the text,[10] it is closer to the rhythms of colloquial speech and in its brush with tragedy it has the power to touch the emotions. Kafka believed that a book could act as an ice-axe to break the sea frozen within us: similarly, this play has the power to evoke an emotional response that can translate into some excellent written work in which language and feeling are closely connected.

Media Work at Key Stage Four – The Way In
Much Ado About Nothing is admirably suited to an approach that begins with a concentration on film and proceeds to dramatic experience. Kenneth Branagh's filmed version provides excellent support to the teacher's task because, although his motives are predominantly commercial rather than educational, Branagh, too, is committed to making an impact on a young audience. With an evangelical zeal for promoting Shakespeare, he follows in the wake of Michael Bogdanov and Franco Zeffirelli, intent on reaching and moving large teenage audiences by making the plays accessible. Baz Luhrmann was to achieve the same feat with his version of *Romeo and Juliet*.

A teacher presenting *Much Ado About Nothing* need only show the opening of Branagh's film version to invoke an atmosphere of anticipation. The tremendous energy and vitality of the homecoming troops, the exuberance of the young women, the breathless pace and sense of festivity in the idyllic Italian sunshine raise the spirits and ensure a positive beginning to a course of study. The film has an instant appeal that facilitates a quick and easy comprehension of the plot.

Branagh reminds us that, nowadays, more people are encountering Shakespeare on film – as neither quite perform-ance nor text – than either in the theatre or in print. He deliberately and unashamedly sets out to give his audiences instant access to the play. In his own words:

In effect, we assumed that no one had seen the play before. We wanted audiences to react to the story as if it were in the here and now and important to them. We did not want them to feel they were in some cultural church.[11]

Once the class has seen the film, both teacher and pupils can be free from this 'cultural church' and ready to begin an analysis of the film text.

The opening sequence revels in the techniques open to a film director, reflecting Branagh's love of cinema in his tribute to *The Magnificent Seven*. There is an extravagant choice of location, imaginative crane-held camera work, a powerful soundtrack and some careful editing of a myriad of shots involving frantic domestic preparation. Nevertheless, as Samuel Crowl comments, by initially concentrating attention on the words of Balthazar's song 'Sigh no more ladies' from Act 2, Scene 3, Branagh can be seen 'balancing one foot on the verbal shore of the play and one in the visual sea of the film.'[12] Branagh, the great promoter of filmed Shakespeare, can here be seen gravitating towards the concerns of the classroom teacher. For while the splendid images of the horsemen seize our visual attention, Emma Thompson's carefully paced reading foregrounds the text, accustoming our ears and eyes to Shakespeare's language and pointing towards the main theme.

Most pupils appreciate the technical accomplishment of this scene. Owing to their familiarity with television and film, they readily display a visual perception and an enthusiasm for learning the relevant media vocabulary. Moreover, with key terms such as 'zoom', 'pan' and 'voice-over' displayed and defined on the classroom wall, they rapidly assimilate the necessary terminology for tackling a media assignment. The range of techniques in the opening and their effects on the tone of the film repay close study. Teachers could either set the task of concentrating on the separate filmic devices that are brought together so magnificently at the beginning, or pupils could be asked to compare the opening of the Branagh film with the more theatrical BBC version.[13] Either exercise would provide them with a useful piece of media coursework designed, according to the GCSE syllabus, to demonstrate their 'ability to analyse, review and comment on features of media texts.'[14]

Approaching the Play
Branagh's *Much Ado About Nothing* works precisely because it contests the long-held critical view that Beatrice and Benedick are the real stars and that 'Hero is a nonentity and Claudio is a cad.'[15] For despite the star casting of Kenneth Branagh and Emma Thompson as the spirited Benedick and vulnerable Beatrice, the film concentrates its dramatic power on the devastating central scene where Claudio rejects Hero as his bride. This inevitably impacts on the sensibilities of a young audience who are emotionally drawn to the younger characters and, in this way, engage with the play at a level of sympathetic personal involvement.

Having observed a class engrossed in the drama, I can vouch for the silent attention and suppression of one or two embarrassed sniffs that Claudio's rejection provokes. In emphasizing a strong sense of hurt and public humiliation, Branagh commits himself to giving 'a different kind of space to the Claudio/Hero plot'.[16] Here, the language of wordplay is deliberately subordinated to the language of feeling. The class will need no footnotes to decipher meaning as they may when disentangling the wit of Beatrice and Benedick. The effect is instant, highlighting Branagh's desire to entertain a young audience by telling the story with the utmost clarity and simplicity. He gets straight to the heart of the drama. His direction of this film could have been aimed at New Town audiences or those with very little experience of watching Shakespeare.

As the NEAB syllabus insists on an 'analysis of the dramatic qualities of one or more scenes',[17] the wedding scene could provide an important focus, even if this means that 'the merry war' of Beatrice and Benedick is relegated to its natural place in the play of subplot. Despite the lively, sparkling, memorable lines, this couple present problems for modern audiences. Consider, for example, the following exchange:

Bene.: Well, you are a rare parrot-teacher.
Beat.: A bird of my tongue is better than a beast of yours.
Bene.: I would my horse had the speed of your tongue, and so good continuer. But keep your way, a God's name, I have done.
Beat.: You always end with a jade's trick, I know you of old.[18]

Beatrice and Benedick are usually presented as the older, more experienced lovers, for as Rossiter points out 'in the game of wit' they see themselves as 'seeded players'.[19] It is, of course, possible to catch their general meaning in a good performance, but a thorough understanding of the incessant punning of their repartee will send pupils to the footnotes to explain the jokes, and an explained joke can lose its effect and even its identity. A pupil at my school once commented, with a sigh of resignation, 'These jokes may have been funny 400 years ago but they aren't funny now.' This, of course, is a controversial point that can be seen to reflect his difficulties with the language rather than any failing in Shakespeare's comic power. Unquestionably, more able pupils of wider intellectual backgrounds would appreciate the wittier elements of the play but, in general, my pupils find greater points of identification with the younger, more artless Claudio and Hero.

It is these characters who experience the sharp pains of betrayal and public humiliation. In Branagh's film, Claudio becomes the 'hurt fowl', whose sense of outrage and pain is so evident in his rejection of Hero that it is possible to retain some sympathy for him in the final scenes of the film. Like him, although with the benefit of dramatic irony, we have witnessed, in Branagh's version the full horror of Margaret posing as Hero in the lascivious balcony scene. It is impossible to dismiss him as gullible. Hero, too, undergoes her painful fate, expressing an innocence and sense of nightmare that affects the atmosphere like a darkening maelstrom, resulting in both a sympathetic and empathetic response from other characters and the audience. This point in the play arouses strong feelings of instinctive alarm, sympathy and disgust.

Structurally, the major currents flow into and out of this scene. It is the vortex of the play, the hub of the wheel, and, as such, a superb scene for close study. All of the principal characters are concerned in Hero's condemnation or defence. Here, the play veers towards disaster as the comic voices of the play are momentarily drowned by the tones of tragedy. From this scene, the comedy has to regain its balance through forgiveness and reconciliation. The issues are grave and open to debate. The sunny atmosphere of Messina has been blackened by slander and the public humiliation of an innocent girl. The insults are gross. The maligned Hero is rejected and verbally abused by both her lover and her father. Such a scene exemplifies the role of women as property and the way in which men could treat them in Renaissance England.

To appreciate the importance of the action, the pupils need to participate in a dramatic interpretation. Most pupils relish a literal approach that includes a physical expression of the text, but it should be understood that a dramatic reconstruction of the church scene is much more than an acting exercise. For while encouraging a thorough understanding of character and language, it can be a prologue to more abstract, literary involvement.

A teacher could begin by using specific concrete objects to symbolize the characters. One way to introduce them would be to draw them individually from a large bag and ask which characters are suggested: an able group could, of course, produce their own assembly of objects. The following are offered as suggestions:

- a pair of spectacles for Leonato;
- gold braid to denote Pedro's rank;
- a rotten orange for Claudio;
- a wedding veil for Hero;
- a black mask for Don John;
- a handkerchief for the weeping Beatrice;
- a crucifix for the friar;
- a sword for Benedick as this scene commits him to revenge.

With these items, the class could begin a mapping exercise, staging or positioning the symbols on a large plan of the stage. Some could read the whole scene, while others plot the movements of the objects; or alternatively the teacher could identify four or five quotations and ask for visual representations of the characters' positions at these points. Through discussion

and negotiation, the pupils will, in this way, begin to appreciate objectively the structure and physical development of the
scene before they take on the roles that give them the further
dimension of empathizing with the characters. According to
Henning Krabbe, they need to come to terms with

> the play viewed as a scenic build-up in which the action
> of the text is only one element, but where also position-
> ing, grouping, movement, costumes . . . use of silence or
> sound or music, have to be taken into account.[20]

This scene is particularly complex, as it twists and turns to
reveal and develop character, while opening out to embrace
the major currents of the whole play.

Once pupils have participated in a performance that is
reasonably fluent and articulate and conscious of the importance of staging, it is possible to introduce an interviewer. In
this role, the teacher, perhaps, can bring to the surface any
emotions engendered by the action and highlight the significance of particular speeches. Accordingly, he or she can
pinpoint key moments by 'freezing' the action into a series of
tableaux in order to question the actors and the audience.
Pupils, both in and out of role, can be encouraged to explore
their reactions and to consider possible consequences to this
scene. The teacher might, for example, stimulate discussion
using a 'What if' approach. 'What if Claudio does not discover
the truth?' 'What if Benedick and Claudio fight a duel?' 'What
if Hero cannot forgive?'

In my experience, pupils readily take on the personae of the
characters and, once nudged into oracy, they begin to extem-
porize using quotations from Shakespeare as part of their own
language. A boy, in role as Leonato, for example, once effort-
lessly declaimed, 'It's like she's stained and useless. She's fallen

into "a pit of ink" and she'll never be clean again. She has dishonoured me because I am her father.' Feeling, expression and quotation are here intimately and naturally connected, forming an excellent preparation for writing.

In all discussions about Hero's public humiliation, feelings of anger generally swell to the point of outrage. Pupils will rigorously interrogate and upbraid characters in the manner of an American chat show. A 'suspension of disbelief' is so easily achieved that it is usually the teacher's task to chair a discussion by calming the situation, linking the points to the text and ensuring that most contributions build a challenging experience from which to reflect and write. The 'freeze' command is invaluable here. If any altercations are too hysterical, or if the discussion seems to be veering off track, the teacher can 'refreeze' the scene and move the play on to the next significant moment.

Another enjoyable dramatic device that could be used to examine the effect of this scene is for the class to stage a 'morning after' breakfast television forum. Here again, some of the pupils can appear seated in a row at the front of the class to answer questions from a studio audience or to be part of a 'phone-in'. The teacher, acting as presenter and interviewer, again has the autonomy to explore particular themes and nuances, focusing attention on pertinent points while tactfully correcting or editing out irrelevant discursive material.

By choosing only a few key moments, the teacher highlights the importance of being selective, a skill that can translate into essay writing and give a direction for further research. Some pupils, for example, may be interested in focusing on Hero's treatment at the hands of Claudio, Pedro and Leonato. They could concentrate on their speeches by examining the language of insult and researching contemporary attitudes towards honour. In this way, they would appreciate the importance of reputation and the part played by Renaissance women in defining the honour of their fathers and husbands.[21] Moreover, researching the reasons behind Claudio's assumption of the moral high ground would give them a fascinating perspective on Elizabethan sexual politics, while at the same time satisfying NEAB's demands for candidates of English Literature

> . . . to demonstrate awareness of social and historical influences, cultural contexts and literary traditions which shaped Shakespeare's writing.[22]

Alternatively, other pupils may wish to approach this scene by concentrating on the powerful effects of deception. Beginning with a study of the 'misprision' of Pedro and Claudio, they could track back through the play, concentrating on the way in which they have been deceived and considering any textual detail that illuminates the nature of their relationship. They could also research Elizabethan attitudes to male friendship and to courtship rituals – my pupils have surprised me by finding the practice of wooing by proxy or using a go-between in a love affair 'cool' and relevant to their own relationships.

For an even wider angle, they could consider the original Bandello story, in which the mature Claudio figure Sir Timbreo shows far more courtesy and consideration to the heroine's father Lionato.[23] Armed with this knowledge, they will inevitably question Shakespeare's dramatic design in making Claudio younger, giving him Pedro as a companion and making him exhibit such despicable behaviour. Having analysed in this way, they can return to the scene to synthesize their findings by setting them beside the perceptive response of the friar and the instinctive gasp of Beatrice's 'On my soul my cousin is belied!' (VI.I.146)

By concentrating on this scene in performance and through

oral simulations, pupils can appreciate the dramatic concerns and empathize with the characters' dilemmas. Through discussion and role-play, they can be encouraged to express and analyse their response in a way that develops the 'understanding and engagement' that are reiterated and seen as central to NEAB's syllabus where Shakespeare is concerned. Branagh's film provides them with an excellent example of a cinematic imagination and leads them to experience the emotion of the play. A dramatic reconstruction of Act 4, Scene 1 facilitates entry into staging, language and character, giving an enthusiastic teacher scope to develop the role of interviewer or benevolent interrogator. In the best lessons, where the teacher is flexible, the group's interests and preoccupations will influence the direction of the course of study, but it can be seen that there are opportunities for inspired groups or individuals to follow the more scholarly paths of close textual examination and further research.

Strong writing flows from thorough preparation. Eventually, many pupils should be able to write eloquently about the importance of this scene, carefully tracing the themes in other parts of the play, including details about the historical context and showing an easy familiarity with the language that enables them to use quotations effectively. Freed from the demands of a written examination under timed conditions, they invariably take pride in their coursework unit for Shakespeare by volunteering to redraft it several times. Many conceive an affection for the play that outlives the programme of lessons, for when asked to return copies of *Much Ado About Nothing*, they will ask to buy them.

New Town pupils are not easy to motivate. Apart from their poor command of Standard English, they can be labelled as confrontational or 'difficult' and be preoccupied by a range of problems in their home backgrounds. The media abounds with distressing images of dilapidated property and poorly-maintained schools in areas where petty crime is an everyday occurrence. Even the statistics reflect their problems: for example, a relatively high proportion of pupils at my school is entitled to free school meals, and this fact alone acts as an indicator to the social problems of financial deprivation and single parenthood. The prospect of studying Shakespeare or anything else at university is a serious option for only a tiny minority.

A middle-class teacher, arriving from one of the surrounding leafy suburbs, has much to do. Enthusiasm and appealing material are desirable but not enough. The task of giving these pupils 'ownership' of Shakespeare texts in a way that develops them is much more challenging. But with an imaginative programme of lessons that takes account of their interests and draws on their strengths, it is possible for pupils to make significant progress as articulate thinkers and writers. At both key stages, they should be encouraged to develop confidence and a belief in their own ability. They must be taught to sharpen their perception, make choices and to aim for the high standards of written work that will ensure examination success. This, in turn, should enable them to reappraise themselves, for despite all their disadvantages and the seeming irrelevance of Shakespeare to their lives, they have much to offer and considerable potential as students of literature.

Notes

1. Rex Gibson, *Teaching Shakespeare*, (Cambridge University Press, 1998), p. xii.
2. Margreta de Grazia, 'Shakespeare and the Craft of Language', in *The Cambridge Companion to Shakespeare*, eds Margreta de Grazia and Stanley Wells, (Cambridge University Press, 2001), p. 51.

3. Frank Kermode, *Shakespeare's Language*, (Allen Lane, Penguin Press, 2000), p. 4.

4. *Ibid.*, Preface, p. vii.

5. Michael Dobson, 'Shakespeare on the stage and on the page', in *The Cambridge Companion to Shakespeare*, eds Margareta de Grazia and Stanley Wells, (Cambridge University Press, 2001) p. 235.

6. Written by Terry Deary and published by Scholastic Publications Ltd, 1998.

7. Frank Kermode, *Shakespeare's Language*, (Allen Lane, Penguin Press, 2000), p. 203.

8. Quoted in *The Bedford Companion to Shakespeare* by Russ Mcdonald, (Bedford Books of St. Martin's Press, 1996), p. 160.

9. George T. Wright, 'Hearing Shakespeare's Dramatic Verse', reprinted in *A Companion to Shakespeare*, ed. David Scott Kastan (Blackwell Publishers Ltd, 1999), p. 272.

10. Frank Kermode, *Shakespeare's Language*, (Allen Lane, Penguin Press, 2000), p. 77. See also D. L. Stevenson's introduction to the Signet edition of *Much Ado About Nothing* (1964), p. xxiii, in which he comments on the mimetic realism partly created by the 'potency of the language'.

11. Kenneth Branagh, *Much Ado About Nothing by William Shakespeare*, (W. W. Norton, 1993), p. ix.

12. Samuel Crowl in 'Flamboyant Realist: Kenneth Branagh', reprinted in *The Cambridge Companion to Shakespeare on Film*, ed. Russell Jackson, (Cambridge University Press, 2000), p. 225.

13. Kenneth Rothwell's detailed explanation of the camera work in *A History of Shakespeare on Screen* (Cambridge University Press, 1999, pp. 250–3) could be used as background to this work.

14. *NEAB English Syllabus 1111*, published by the Northern Examining Board for 2001 and 2002, p. 17.

15. Kenneth Muir, *Shakespeare's Comic Sequence,* (Liverpool University Press, 1979), p. 72.

16. Kenneth Branagh, *Much Ado About Nothing by William Shakespeare,* (W. W. Norton, 1993), p. vii.

17. *NEAB English Syllabus 1111,* published by the Northern Examining Board for 2001 and 2002, p. 15.

18. *Much Ado About Nothing* Act 1, Scene 1 lines 127–34.

19. A. P. Rossiter, *Angel With Horns* (Longman, 1961), p. 69.

20. Reprinted in the introduction to *The Arden Shakespeare: Much Ado About Nothing,* ed. A. R. Humphreys (Methuen, 1981), p. 60.

21. See S. P. Ceserano's essay 'Half a Dozen Dangerous Words' pages 31–50 in *New Casebooks, Much Ado About Nothing and The Taming of the Shrew,* ed. Marion Wynne-Davis (Palgrave, 2001).

22. *NEAB English Syllabus 1111,* published by the Northern Examining Board for 2001 and 2002, p. 15.

23. See Michael Gearin-Tosh's essay 'The World of Much Ado About Nothing', in *Critical Essays on Much Ado About Nothing,* eds Linda Cookson and Bryan Loughrey, (Longman, 1989).

CHAPTER 4

Shakespeare at Eton College

Joseph Francis

> Not marble, nor the gilded monuments
> Of princes, shall outlive this powerful rhyme.
> (Sonnet 55)

In the first scene of *Henry VI Part I*, a wary Gloucester speaks
with the Bishop of Winchester, describing the uncrowned king
as 'an effeminate prince, / Whom, like a schoolboy, you may
overawe'. Although it takes three plays to finish him off, in the
end Henry is indeed overawed, overwhelmed and undone;
losing, along the way, the French territories conquered by his
more illustrious father. His story, whether told by Hall, Holinshed, or by Shakespeare himself, has a particular resonance at
Eton College: the vulnerable and scholarly Henry VI was
responsible for founding us.

Eton College, then, is an historical sort of place. Heathrow
airport provides a rude reminder every ninety seconds that the
twenty-first century is underway (at least overhead), but many
of the school's rituals, much of its jargon and most of its principal buildings are the legacy of previous centuries. In such a
context, it is worth remembering that the subject of English is
a relatively recent invention – very much a twentieth-century
phenomenon. Indeed, in that Eton came into existence long

Figure 1: *Theatricals in Long Chamber*, watercolour, Samuel Evans c.1815.
(The play in performance would appear to be *A Midsummer Night's Dream*.)

before the birth of Shakespeare, it is significant that its fundamental curriculum endured unchanged for hundreds of years after his death. It did not fully and formally introduce the study of his writing, or of English Literature in general, until 1963 – much later than most educational establishments in the English-speaking world. This is not to say that before then Etonians were somehow insulated from Shakespeare. It is true that the original statutes of the College frown upon drama, and true also that boys were banned from putting on plays from 1870 until the end of the First World War. However, the imposition of this dark age came about precisely because of the popularity of drama among the boys – something that made the authorities uneasy. Clandestine 'theatricals' had been staged in dormitories and even hired inn rooms from the middle of the eighteenth century. Plays by Fielding and Sheridan were especially popular, but Shakespeare was also performed: perhaps predominantly in abridged forms, tailored, as in the case of *A Midsummer Night's Dream*, in favour of the comic highlights. In short, Shakespeare was entertainment at Eton College long before he was education.

But while the formal curriculum of Eton's schoolrooms may have excluded Shakespeare, traditionally there was always a second, less formal educational context called 'private business', when groups of boys visited the homes of their tutors. What tutors did in this time varied considerably, but in the nineteenth century we know that English literature, while perhaps not *taught* in a way we would recognize, was certainly read and discussed with boys by progressive figures such as William Johnson. By the 1890s, when the Strafford Shakespeare Medal was introduced, boys were being examined on their knowledge of his plays; and the 1920s, as anyone familiar with *The Lyttelton Hart-Davis Letters* will know, saw the introduction of an optional (but very popular) English Literature course for senior boys taught by George Lyttelton. That Lyttelton was a classicist by training reminds us that literary minds are not exclusively possessed by English teachers.

Thus, on the one hand, Eton was slow to respond to the twentieth-century trends in education which made English Literature such a prominent subject; while on the other, one reason for this slowness was the perception that this educational need was already being addressed in less formal contexts.

But as they wrestle with his plays at GCSE and A-level in much the same way as students anywhere else, perhaps today's Etonians are less inclined to associate Shakespeare with pleasure than their predecessors were. It is a mischievous reflection, but if one's educational diet were dominated by Classics, Divinity and Mathematics, going to see your school fellows perform *Twelfth Night* or *Macbeth* must have been a different kind of experience than it could be today, now that such plays are set texts. Likewise, perhaps a Shakespeare sonnet would be treasured and absorbed more sincerely when it was encountered in the study of an enlightened tutor, rather than in a prescribed anthology or an examination. It is a provoking thought, also, that a distinguished Old Etonian like John Barton, who went on to direct at the RSC, would scarcely have recognized the subject of English as it is now taught and examined. What Eton did give him, however, was the opportunity to direct Shakespeare: he produced a celebrated *Henry IV Part I* in 1947 (in which Douglas Hurd played Worcester). Even if Barton was an exception rather than a rule, we may conclude that the cultivation of a sensibility which can direct Shakespeare at the highest level does not depend on 'doing him' at A-level.

Shakespeare should be presented as what he was, an entertainer – a word which need not have trivial connotations.

Perhaps the greatest impediment to doing this effectively is that fact of his also being a heavily prescribed set author. The challenge at Eton is the same as everywhere else: both to teach his works and to let them entertain. It is an essential but tricky balance to strike. At Eton, I have no doubt that one lifeline which makes this balance attainable is the vibrancy of school theatre. Nevertheless, precisely because English Literature as an academic subject is founded upon sources of recreation and entertainment, namely good books, it is important to acknowledge that there are dangers in teaching it which no other subject faces in quite the same way.

I am not alone among English teachers at Eton in feeling that while I want my students to associate what we read together with pleasure, I suspect that too often they associate it with the pressure of examinations and coursework. Nor can I really blame them for doing so. And rather than cultivating the love of reading or theatre, I sometimes suspect, in a dark and guilty corner of my heart, that I am part of a national system which is rapidly evolving in a way which threatens to undermine this objective. One of the great propagandists for Shakespeare, Samuel Taylor Coleridge, insisted 'He is of no age': it would certainly be a great pity if students of the present or the future were to resist this notion of enduring appeal. But Coleridge also wrote, in his poem *The Three Graves*, 'We ne'er can be / Made happy by compulsion'.

However, there is no member of the English department at Eton who would not wish to teach Shakespeare. Given that he is the only compulsory author in the National Curriculum, this is fortunate, particularly as the principle that individual teachers should be able to choose which authors and texts they teach is one which our department upholds vigorously. This principle has survived the implementation of modular A-levels, and is only restricted by the variety of choice offered by the examination board. So no other authors are prescribed by our department: there is no stipulation to teach Chaucer, Milton, Wordsworth, Dickens or any particular twentieth-century writer. Admittedly, there is a strong likelihood that an Etonian who continued with the subject through AS and A2 would come across one or more other such 'major authors', but there is no internal monitoring to guarantee this. Nor is there a requirement that even one female author will be studied, or that our students will at some point cast their eyes over the work of Fielding, Gray, Shelley, Swinburne, Orwell or Huxley – Eton's best known literary alumni.

Shakespeare is the exception. One of his plays will be taught before GCSE to thirteen-year-olds in their first year here, another during GCSE (for coursework) to fifteen-year-olds. For those who continue with the subject (usually about a third of the 250 or so boys in each year), another play is taught for examination at AS, and many teachers have chosen to teach a further Shakespeare text in the A2 year. It might be argued that this demonstrates a certain inertia – a reluctance, perhaps, to explore lesser-known texts on the A2 drama syllabus. I think it more likely, however, that teachers are teaching Shakespeare at A2 because they want to, and because there is no perception of resistance to these choices among our students.

Thus, while Shakespeare is undeniably and emphatically prescribed, it might be more truthful to say, at Eton anyway, that he occupies a realm beyond prescription. What we do is certainly in line with the requirements of examination boards and curriculum authorities, but it is supplemented by features of our own making, not just in this continued preference at A2, but in other things too: a Shakespeare declamation prize in the first year, a Shakespeare essay prize for sixth formers, a Shakespeare Society and so forth.

Indeed, reflecting on Shakespeare's description of Henry VI as an overawed schoolboy, it occurs to me that there is ample opportunity for Eton's schoolboys to be overawed by Shakespeare. And yet, unlike that other literary schoolboy in Blake's *Songs of Experience* (who endures 'many an anxious hour' confined 'in learning's bower'), it would seem that Shakespeare is not perceived as a challenge rather than an imposition.

What's past is prologue . . .

Although Shakespeare's status is enshrined within the academic subject of English Literature, it does not follow that it therefore depends on our subject. The historical perspectives which Eton affords certainly remind us that Shakespeare has not become a pervasive cultural influence purely because he is taught in schools.

Cultural materialism offers compelling arguments (outlined in Robert Eaglestone's recent guide, *Doing English*) for questioning the legitimacy of Shakespeare's domination of the syllabus. It is possible to demonstrate that political, cultural and economic interests have played a crucial role in establishing the hegemony of Shakespeare. Indeed, the concept of 'first mover advantage', used by economists with reference to corporations like Microsoft, can be provocatively applied to explain why he has become an 'industry standard' in English education. But despite the cherished objectivity of cultural materialism, in the case of Shakespeare its arguments can acquire a conspiratorial flavour – as if unveiling the insidious forces that have bound us against our will.

For cultural materialists interested in educational tyranny, there can be few better examples than Eton College itself – though not, I hope, as it is presently constituted. I have already alluded to the narrow curricular regimes of the past. While these were comparable to those offered by many institutions, and compensated for to some degree by extra-curricular tutorials and the influence of figures like Johnson and Lyttelton, it is doubtful whether Eton can be said ever to have been a progressive school, or boast of having been an enlightened and cultured establishment throughout its history. This fact makes it all the more significant that Shakespeare was an influence and inspiration to students long before they would have had instruction in English Literature. In 1818, when Winthrop Mackworth Praed was at Eton, he wrote a comic play called *Robin Hood*. It included numerous burlesques of Shakespeare. In the following extract, Little John, having mounted the table in a tavern scene reminiscent of *Henry IV Part I*, boasts of how he beat up Robin's rival, Riquet:

> This is my answer, not that I loved Riquet less, but that I loved myself more. As Riquet was a fellow rogue, I loved him, as he was a wag, I laughed at him; as he was drunk, I quarrelled with him; and as he jawed I thrashed him. There is love for his roguery, laughter for his waggery, a quarrel for his drunkenness, and a thrashing for his jaw.

Here, Brutus' forum speech from *Julius Caesar* is clearly in Praed's mind. Elsewhere in his play, *Hamlet*, *Othello*, *Macbeth* and even *Henry VIII* provide models which his characters spoof. Not bad for a fifteen-year-old.

It would be wrong to present Praed as a representative nineteenth-century Etonian. Nevertheless, no writer performs in a vacuum. If Praed intended to delight his audience, as I'm sure he did, he must have known they would recognize his sources of parody. We can be sure that Praed and many of his contemporaries saw Shakespeare performed in London, and by actors as distinguished as Macready and Kean. We also know that copies of Shakespeare were given as leaving presents, and the growth of the publishing industry in the eighteenth century would have played a part in the wider availability of his work to the reading public. Thus Shakespeare was very much a part of the cultural awareness of educated young men, even when, strictly speaking, he was not a part of their education (although it would misrepresent the concept of a gentleman's education at the time to say that it was confined by the parameters of school lessons).

It is worth noting that almost every edition of Shakespeare is now produced with an eye on the educational marketplace; again, this reflects a shift from the private consumption of his writings to their primary use today as an educational tool. Praed's formal education may well have contributed, particularly through exercises in Latin and Greek versification, to the rhetorical and metrical fluency of his extra-curricular 'creative writing'. But whereas today's Etonians are most likely to read their Shakespeare in an educational context, Praed demonstrates that Shakespeare's influence transcended the educational criteria of his time.

It is perhaps apt to offer a comparison with a recent Etonian whose writing also reflects a Shakespearean influence. The highlight of the School Play Festival of 1999 was *Kassandra* by Ivo Stourton, then in his final year at Eton. Its ingredients were Greek tragedy, the Vietnam War and American infantrymen speaking in blank verse. The following extract is spoken by the character Smoker, a drug-dealing GI whose wares, although lyrically advertised here, induce insanity and blindness:

Something stronger then? I have in my bag
Such kindling tabs as will ignite his soul
To burn inferno brighter than the sun
And blind his tired sight to light cast by

THE ARTS REVIEW

School Play Festival Special Free Edition   October 15th 1999

Gooks A Go-Go

Andrew Grenfell, our very own war correspondent, returns from the front (row) to report **Ivo Stourton's** *Kassandra*, directed by **H-EO**.

A smoke-filled Empty Space proved the ideal venue to create the powerful and realistic feel of a U.S. Army camp in Vietnam. The play was a tremendous achievement, not only on the part of the actors, who brought great feeling and power to the story, but also by the author. Blank verse is not easy to pull off, and is easy to ridicule when it doesn't work, but the cast used it with natural grace and controlled the tempo of the language. Accents were perhaps a slight flaw among the male cast, who nevertheless put up a valiant effort to hold on to their Southern drawls. The actress playing Kassandra, it must be said, kept up a solid French accent throughout.

Individual characters were very convincing, with Adetomiwa Edun and Beau Hopkins both extremely powerful on stage. Though not tall, Edun had enormous dramatic stature, and managed to dominate much larger characters realistically and effectively. Hopkins, as Lancaster, was very convincing as an officer racked by resentment but who needs a cause to live or die for. Nyasha Hatendi as Brutal, and Ned Barrie as Smoker

were also extremely powerful presences who dominated their scenes. Frost, played by John Rogerson, is in some ways the most interesting character – a window through which the play can be viewed as he learns of the corruption of war and what the reality of the situation is at the cost of his pacifism. But all the performances were powerful and convincing. The movement and the declamation of the actors, who often had to conduct dialogue at shouting level, were always admirable.

Much of the style is borrowed from Shakespeare, and there are frequent hints of *Henry VI* and *Romeo and Juliet*. However, there is also a contrast with the short, pithy exclamations American soldiers would have used at the time. In places, this provides light relief but for the most part it gives serious emphasis to the juxtaposition of time and place. The grander Shakesperian monologues prove to be surprisingly moving, often coming between bursts of action. They add an extra psychological dimension to the play, reminiscent of *A Thin Red Line*, as well as a surreal quality as the characters seem to be exploring themselves in between the brilliantly choreographed fight scenes.

Punctuated throughout with music of the Vietnam era, the performance closes with the cast dancing on stage, a departure from the traditional curtain call – but this is not, after all, a traditional sort of play.

REMAINING PERFORMANCES (CHIT ONLY) SATURDAY 5.00; SUNDAY 8.15. EMPTY SPACE.

Figure 2: *The Arts Review (School Play Festival Free Edition)*, 1999. (*The Arts Review*, one of several boy-edited magazines at Eton, reviews school productions regularly both in print and on its website.)

His anger or his love. I am a priest
Of sorts and if he will embrace my faith
The Goddess Mary-Jane will fill his lungs
To bursting point with all that's worth the while
And wile away the time in holy quest
To seize the blue dragon, to live in realms
Of colour and of light. The road he takes
Of melancholy contemplation of
The future and the past, what road is that?
It doubles back in riddles and in lies
And does a dance too quick for mortal eyes.

Stourton was partly inspired by plays like Berkoff's *East* and *Greek*, combining modern verse idiom with a classical source, but the metre here is overtly Shakespearian. Yet this is not the kind of attempt which embarrasses an audience, or prompts a pedantic lament (from stuffed shirts such as myself) about the death of verse drama. *Kassandra*, performed with belting vigour and given the assistance of excellent direction, lighting and costume (as well as bangs, smoke and backing tracks from Hendrix), really did work. It demonstrated that the challenge of metre and form is neither beyond contemporary teenagers nor incompatible with genuine dramatic resonance. Perhaps it also demonstrated that while films such as *Apocalypse Now*, *Full Metal Jacket* and *The Thin Red Line* are a potent cultural influence, their language may not offer stylistic models which carry the force of emotion – the poetry – which young writers sometimes wish to convey.

Shakespeare's language does. It was no coincidence that the School Play the previous year had been an abridged and accelerated version of the *Henry VI* sequence, in modern dress, in which Stourton himself had performed. (And no, although you might suspect the performance of the *Henry VI* plays to be an annual ritual – a feature of Founder's Day, perhaps – this was the first ever seen at Eton.) The language, the pace and, it must be said, the gore of that production grabbed the imagination of audience and participants alike.

Between Praed and Stourton, the nature of education has changed almost unimaginably. Moreover, the evolution of our national – and now global – culture has profoundly affected the experience of being a teenager. To Praed and his contemporaries, even to John Barton, Shakespeare was essentially a diversion– for the true enthusiasts, perhaps a kind of hobby. For Ivo Stourton's generation, it must be conceded that other media and stimuli have gone some way towards eclipsing that perception of Shakespeare.

It is reassuring then to see that some common ground can still be discovered across the centuries: common ground which, at least in this comparison, centres on Shakespeare. And to some extent, creative writing – or, more accurately, writing done for pleasure and personal fulfilment outside the set curriculum – may offer a better gauge of Shakespeare's true influence. No one compelled Praed or Stourton to write their plays, or to incorporate the Shakespearian dimension evident in both. Moreover, in that he studied English at both GCSE and A-level, Stourton was obliged to write essays on Shakespeare. To me, this makes the accomplishment of *Kassandra* even more heartening, and demonstrates that compulsory academic study need not inhibit a creative response.

If this were played upon a stage . . .

Recently I taught *Titus Andronicus* to a GCSE set. After a few weeks of bloodshed and retribution, when I was becoming resigned to the fact that my rather perverse selection of a rather perverse play would produce some rather perverse coursework, it emerged that two of the class were taking part in their boarding house's production of *Coriolanus* being staged later that term. One of them had a small supporting part, but the other was playing Aufidius, general to the Volscians (and looking forward to wearing furry boots). It was the turning point of that teaching experience because, quite suddenly, it opened up comparisons between the dark and steely natures of Titus and Coriolanus and their shifting status as insiders and outsiders in the politics of Rome – comparisons I had not supposed available at that level of discourse. The two actors wrote especially well because of their experience; perhaps more importantly, they contributed to a wider reappraisal of the teaching text which enlivened the responses of everyone in the set – particularly because they were able to go and see *Coriolanus* for themselves.

A fortuitous occurrence such as this does not happen every year, but it is an example of the educational dividends which can spring from immediate personal engagement in theatre. It is also a reason why the integration of English and Drama is a healthy thing: in my view, a necessary thing, and particularly so in the presence of Shakespeare. To state that Shakespeare wrote his plays for performance and not for literary study is axiomatic. And yet the practice of English teaching, and particularly desk-bound teaching for coursework and exams, inevitably drifts (if desks can drift) away from the stage and towards text. I was reminded of this at a recent briefing for AS examiners, where we were exhorted to reward Shakespeare candidates generously if they offered observations about staging or demonstrated a knowledge of different productions. The exhortation was appropriate and in many ways reassuring, but the fact that it was necessary says much about the frame of mind in which many teachers, myself included, instinctively engage with their well-thumbed editions of his works.

Marking Shakespeare essays, one often circles dopey phrases like 'the book' and 'the reader', writing in the margin 'play!' and 'audience!' with increasing indignation. Even at Eton, where Shakespeare is regularly in performance, it is very easy for students to see the theatrical process as a subsidiary issue. Moreover, perhaps the criteria by which we mark essays also serves to distance Shakespeare from the stage. Our primary concerns as English teachers are with language (that of both the author and the student) and, I think still, with characters. Increasingly these days, our next concern is often with critical perspectives and historical context. Thus, students whose essays discuss Shakespeare's texts novelistically, showing a grasp of character and situation, can just about scrape by; if they can then demonstrate sensitivity to language and poetry, they begin to do well. If, in addition, they throw in some pertinent details about kingship, or sources, or something gleaned from critical reading, their essays will invariably win a simpering endorsement from the teacher. But examination candidates are not necessarily regarded as surpassing these approaches, or compensating for their absence, by exploring the dramatic variables which can affect the perceptions of an audience. And while literature teachers usually cherish the potential of text to carry diverse meanings, they can be less comfortable with theatrical ideas which have a more tentative relationship with the text – the kind that might work on stage better than they would in an essay.

In examining how theatre affects the way students respond to text, it might be worthwhile to consider the problem of how we get them to professional productions. For a school nestled cosily between the M3 and the M25, it is amazingly difficult to get a whole class, let alone a whole year group, from Eton to a London theatre. Boys have afternoon and evening commitments to a plethora of activities: in fact, they are more likely to go to the theatre in a smaller tutorial outing than with the English Department. (Again, even today, the role of tutors outside the formal curriculum is often culturally invaluable.)

A canny curricular solution was hit upon when, noticing that A-level students doing other subjects regularly went on 'Field Trips', the English Department decided to attempt a jaunt of their own – to Stratford-upon-Avon. Now, in their AS year, all boys studying English are taken off for a two-day course: usually to see two Shakespeare productions at the RSC, between which they visit some of the key museums and properties, hear a lecture on performance history, participate in a drama workshop and attend an open-floor discussion with a member of the cast they have seen. It does not matter that the plays are unlikely to correspond with those they are studying for examination: in fact, in terms of the breadth of their experience of Shakespeare, this is preferable. When they return to Eton, quite as shattered as they would have been after an expedition to survey drainage patterns in the Pennines, the hope is that they see Shakespeare as a writer of drama, not just of set texts.

But for young people, the experience of watching or participating in School Drama is perhaps as educationally important as seeing plays performed on the professional stage, principally because it heightens awareness about the unstable relationship between theatre and text. In the case of Shakespeare, obviously the opportunity to see a professional production can make an invaluable contribution to study; and if this is not possible, a good film version can compensate to a considerable extent (and at Eton we are lucky to have an excellent and varied provision of video sources in School Library). However, it is perhaps important to recognize that when a Shakespeare student, even in the Sixth Form, sees either a professional play or a film for the first time, this will often be perceived as in some way a definitive interpretation of the text. It requires habitual theatre-going before we, as adults, are able to furnish comparisons from our own experience which enable us to see any staged or filmed version of a Shakespeare play as provisional and exploratory. As for films, because screen culture is so powerful, students may even regard filmed Shakespeare as somehow being an improvement on the text; and because they are just as likely to see the screen adaptation of a novel as they are that of a play, films do not necessarily enhance the perception of Shakespeare as drama, as opposed to being a 'book'.

School productions, anywhere, can be excellent or diabolical. But they do have one particular advantage in that rarely, if ever, are they perceived to offer a touchstone or paradigm of the way a text is 'meant' to be performed. In that the notion of a definitive production is, in any case, erroneous, this means that both those who take part and those who watch are undeceived by the experience: young actors learn that there are different ways of doing things, a young audience is aware that they are witnessing an attempt rather than a demonstration. Some things come off, some things don't: doers and watchers alike can puzzle over why. And in the chat and opinion which spreads around a school, both prior to and during a production, much consideration is given to primitive but purposeful questions such as whether a play is good or bad in itself, and how the production in progress measures up to or reflects its quality. Such discussion among boys here (while much of it may be slanderous and ill informed) at least fosters the understanding that theatre is converted from text and that this process is both fraught with risk and pregnant with possibility.

As You Like It, the School Play for Michaelmas 2001, provided an example of a production where the director's strategy was all the more tangible and provocative because of its context at Eton. In adopting the Shakespearian convention of the all-male cast – not unusual here, for obvious reasons – the comic dimension of the play was enhanced because it addressed, and took seriously, parodies both of femininity and masculinity. The phenomenon of a seventeen year-old boy playing a girl (Rosalind) playing a boy (Ganymede) playing a girl ('Rosalind') could not have better accentuated the gender mirrors Shakespeare was exploring. Boys in an all-male boarding environment are very sensitive to these nuances, both because they perceive a peculiar set of pressures pertaining to their own masculinity and because the stage is the unique context at Eton in which girls – brought in from neighbouring schools – can usually be seen alongside boys. Thus the production offered both an atavistic vision of Shakespeare and a contemporary view of Eton.

Another example of how an Eton production has stimulated an awareness of dramatic strategies and variables is in the casting of black actors. We live in an age of 'transparent' ethnicity on the professional Shakespeare stage, in which sometimes we are not supposed to notice that an English king or a Scottish warlord is black or Jewish. In a 1999 house production of *Twelfth Night*, we saw a black actor in the part of Malvolio. In keeping with his character, he projected a grumpy and self-important isolation – an isolation accentuated by the colour of his skin. I remember discussing the production with students studying *Much Ado About Nothing*, whom I had asked to read *Othello* as a supporting text. It was they, not I, who decided that this Malvolio offered intriguing comedic parallels to the predicament of Shakespeare's Moor: a pompous, insecure man delighted by the idea that a beautiful, well-born white girl could love him, an idea which others find absurd, and which is used, through pranks and gulling, to bring about his ruin. Although my contemporary instinct was not to notice Malvolio's blackness, I think my students were probably onto something.

My point is that teaching Shakespeare as a classroom text needs to harness some of the adventure that exists in the process of bringing his plays to theatrical life. If Shakespeare as text can be integrated with Shakespeare as drama in an educational context, then I think he and his students will thrive. And what students need to understand more than anything, is that Shakespeare is not a fixed experience but something open to permutation and experimentation. The kind of conjecture which I think helps teaching – and should help writing essays – occurs when we ask questions like 'What if the actor playing Caliban is strikingly handsome?' or 'Does it matter if Gertrude is more or less the same age as Hamlet?' These may not be the kind of questions which pertain directly to the textual experience of Shakespeare (and I am in no sense proposing to suspend rational and judicious examination of the text), but they are questions provoked exclusively by performance, when the letter of the text and the spirit of the text may not be quite the same thing. Good reading does not necessarily mean literal reading, and in any case, the most persuasive and striking directorial decisions usually spring from insightful response to text. Thus, when Olivier played the title role in his 1948 film of *Hamlet*, he was more than ten years older than the actress playing Gertrude. While logically and literally absurd, it was a casting decision that enhanced the sexual chemistry of the closet scene and chimed with many of the signals and preoccupations evident in the text.

Not only do good dramatic ideas spring from good reading; any dramatic idea can at least be said also to send you back to the text to assess its pedigree and persuasiveness. For these reasons alone it seems to me fatal to sever Drama from English – above all, perhaps, where Shakespeare is concerned.

At Eton, admittedly by accident rather than design, the two subjects have become inseparably allied. For this reason it is all the more important (and all the more difficult) to consider the infrastructure and influence of Drama in the way we experience and teach Shakespeare.

Do not saw the air thus . . .

It is always surprising to hear of schools where the English and Drama departments are not integrated. Certainly, examined Drama and Theatre Studies require specialist teaching skills and expertise beyond the province of English and English Literature. Heads of English, too, can sometimes regard as intrusive and unfairly burdensome the expectation that they, or their teaching staff, should take extra-curricular responsibility for putting on plays. At Eton, where around twenty plays are put on each year (excluding mini-spectacles like GCSE shows and House Drama competitions), it would be impossible for the sixteen members of the English Department to direct them all. Directing plays, including plays by Shakespeare, is therefore a responsibility shared across many colleagues teaching many different subjects: and indeed, importantly, something that boys do too on occasion.

Nevertheless, the fact that six full-time members of the English Department teach Drama and that, with one part-time exception, no one who teaches Drama does not also teach English at every level, means there is effectively a complete synthesis between the two – a synthesis that is architectural as well as departmental. Eton's principal School Theatre stands adjacent to the English Department, and was connected to it in 1990 by a three-storey complex housing make-up suites and dressing rooms. Two additional theatre spaces are located within the Department building itself. Of course, these facilities are not devoted week-in and week-out to the production of Shakespeare. Nevertheless, the duration of a boy's career at Eton being five years (in National Curriculum terms, Years 9 to 13), it would seem appropriate to list the Shakespeare productions that have been staged here between 1997 and 2002. As House plays, or plays by independent school companies: *Othello*, *A Midsummer Night's Dream*, *Hamlet*, *Twelfth Night*, *Coriolanus* and *Henry V*. As School Plays: *The Tempest*, *Julius Caesar*, the *Henry VI* trilogy and *As You Like It*.

Considering that *The Duchess of Malfi*, *Doctor Faustus*, *Rosencrantz and Guildenstern are Dead* and *The Spanish Tragedy* have also been performed over this period, Eton could almost be presented as a fanatical outpost of the RSC (with whom our current Director of Drama acted for a number of years). But it would be disingenuous to imply that every boy in the School was clamouring to see each of these productions, or even that every seat in the house was always full. Moreover, while several of these shows were wonderful, others were forgettable and one or two have been unforgettable for all the wrong reasons. What matters is that theatre has become a key part of extra-curricular life at Eton, both for teachers and students. Plays are not so much events in the School Calendar as things that are going on all the time. What is more pertinent from the perspective of teaching English here is that it has become unusual to take an A-level set in which several boys have not been actively involved in a theatre production of some kind. Naturally, a smaller proportion will have acted in Shakespeare, but as the example of *Coriolanus* shows, it can make a big difference when they have.

To some extent, the picture I have offered thus far, in which a profusion of extra-curricular drama and creative writing dovetails with the curricular teaching of Drama, Literature and English, is misleading – a function, perhaps, of my own polemical agenda to promote their integration. Certainly, Shakespeare at Eton is not a phenomenon that can be judiciously anatomized and sub-divided, particularly because so many of the same teachers and students work together in overlapping circumstances on overlapping projects which benefit from such synchronicity. Nevertheless, Drama operates as a discrete and carefully structured curricular subject.

Given that Shakespeare is a dramatist, it is interesting that his plays are not prescribed either at GCSE or at A-level: it might even be appropriate to suggest that he is rather over-prescribed in the subject of English Literature (although not all my colleagues would agree), and rather under-prescribed in Drama. But as it happens, Shakespeare crops up quite prominently, here anyway, on the written side of the Drama courses – it would be unusual for boys not to study a Shakespeare production for coursework or an exam topic. There are three reasons for this, all of which really relate to practicality and none to principle. The first is that, in comparison with more contemporary plays like *The Homecoming* or *Art*, the ideas evident in production design are often much more tangible with Shakespeare shows, and therefore easier for students to evaluate. Second, Shakespeare's performance history is better documented and more accessible, enabling students to discuss the 'relativity' of productions more purposefully (and avoid the aforementioned pitfall of seeing a particular production as definitive). Third, however, it is simply because the orientation of English teaching at Eton means that Shakespeare is not an alien or forbidding experience to most of our students.

These explanations certainly reveal a kind of inescapable 'feedback loop' which brings Shakespeare to the fore even where he is not prescribed. Alternatively, one could say that his pre-eminence in our English curriculum is actually liberating for the teaching of drama: in the same way that Ivo Stourton's creative writing is the product of a comfortable relationship with Shakespeare's language, boys assessing the production merits of a Shakespeare play can do so with an assurance acquired through consistent exposure to his work in the English classroom. And it is with the English classroom – perhaps where I should have begun – that I want to conclude this discussion.

Study what you most affect . . .

To argue that we do not teach Shakespeare at Eton purely because he is prescribed for examination is all very well – and I hope true – but the fact is that what we teach him *for* is almost always examination or coursework.

The only exception is the First Year (Year 9 in the National Curriculum), where texts like *Julius Caesar*, *Henry V*, *Richard III*, *Romeo and Juliet* and *The Tempest* feature prominently. These are regarded, as they probably would be in most schools, as more approachable for thirteen-year-olds – partly, it must be said, because popular films are a key teaching aid. Boys come to Eton with a little bit of prep school Shakespeare and, generally, can be nursed through these texts without too much difficulty in comprehension. We introduce some preliminary skills in literary criticism, but the primary objective is to cultivate engagement and enjoyment, and many written and spoken tasks will be imaginative. If there is an emphasis on studying one whole text rather than a number of Shakespeare extracts, this is because what interests boys at this level is perhaps the plot and the destiny of the characters more than the intricacies of language. But at some point every boy learns and declaims a passage from the text, and the best performer from each of the thirteen sets – the one who captures the sense and spirit of a speech with the most aplomb – goes through to a grand final, which all First Year boys attend. A little bit of showbiz, then, to round off their first taste of Shakespeare here.

The Second Year at Eton (Year 10), during which no Shakespeare is currently studied, is when teachers become more concerned with fostering critical skills at the beginning of the GCSE course. This course is about to change once more – indeed, it is even conceivable that we may not be teaching GCSE at all in a few years time. But at present, and for the foreseeable future, our practice is to return to Shakespeare in the Third Year (Year 11) and study a play in some detail for coursework purposes. By this time, the hope is that boys are more at home with the process of quotation, analysis and argument, as there is now much more emphasis on the nuances of Shakespeare's language. That we defer teaching Shakespeare until the later stages of GCSE seems significant: an acknowledgement that he is perhaps the most difficult and substantial hurdle in the course – in some sense, its climax.

At Eton, it must be said that we have a relatively strong pool of GCSE candidates. This means that it already makes sense to teach with a view to Sixth Form objectives, for the stronger students are writing with the fluency and insight of good A-level candidates, at least in their coursework.

Although Shakespeare examinations are nothing new, their new configuration at A-level seems to have a more intrusive influence on the way we teach. In the past, it was possible to study a Shakespeare play almost for its own sake, knowing that the public examinations were many months away and that there would be time to return to it in the weeks before an exam with a view to sharpening preparation and performance. Today, courses at AS and A2 have to be devised with scrupulous attention to the availability of time. We have been conscious at Eton that a number of schools have sought to defend the introductory status of the first year of the Sixth

Form by, for example, postponing the teaching of examined texts until as late as the second term. This approach is entirely understandable: the wider reading of non-examined texts seems an important platform for progression beyond GCSE. Our concern, however, was that such an approach would inevitably limit the depth of attention that could be paid to set texts, and perhaps above all to Shakespeare, where our general perception is that students need to have a secure line-by-line comprehension before they are ready for examination – especially for extract-based questions.

Moreover, the new assessment objectives, by placing greater emphasis on supplementary issues like historical context, might also be seen as reducing the time that could be devoted to close reading. What we wanted to avoid with Shakespeare was the kind of light textual approach which might encourage students to compensate for a lack of detailed engagement with what characters actually say by focusing, perhaps glibly, on thematic angles, cultural background and titbits from criticism. Of course we have to address these elements too – we hope we always have done – although we do not wish to do so at the expense of close reading. Perhaps our biggest concern as a department is that in the general currents affecting education, the good ship English Literature is in danger of being drawn into the broader, murkier and, to us, less interesting vortex of 'Cultural Studies'. The day has not quite arrived when the examination papers ask, 'How has *The Merchant of Venice* contributed to your understanding of Jewish identity in the sixteenth century?' But there is a danger that the study of literature will become annexed to, or justified by, historical and cultural study.

One of the reasons why close analysis is such an invaluable tool is that it throws up, in its difficult moments, ideas which perplex and provoke the teacher as much as the student. I was picked up last year on some tricky lines in Hamlet's final soliloquy, where his thoughts are prompted by the troop-movements of Fortinbras:

> Rightly to be great
> Is not to stir without great argument,
> But greatly to find quarrel in a straw
> When honour's at the stake.
>
> (4.4. 53–6)

I had always taken these lines to mean something like 'a truly great man will always defend his honour, even over trivial matters'. My students didn't let me get away with that. They pointed out that the reason these lines are difficult to follow is that the first two work very elegantly as an aphorism in their own right, only to be developed, and contradicted rather clumsily, in the two lines which follow. And because of the vowel rhyme between 'great' and 'stake', a curious symmetry and opposition is formed – a paradoxical structure which dramatizes Hamlet's struggle to persuade himself of something he is not sure about.

Perhaps I went into the classroom poorly prepared here, although the experience of being pulled up by one's own students is titillating as much as chastening. Really, the whole excitement of teaching literature hinges on those moments where, as Shelley put it, someone discovers 'a lightning that has yet found no conductor'. And even if these particular electrical sparks in *Hamlet* have long been current in cleverer minds than mine, the newness – in a classroom – need only be felt by the people present to be exhilarating.

This is the danger of spending too much time teaching background about, for example, Renaissance issues of honour or soldiery: you end up missing the detail, which is often where the stimulation lies. Moreover, in a way it is easier to teach general background because one is not exposed to the live scrutiny of students in the way that text, closely and candidly considered, demands. And if the ultimate aim is to get incisive, exciting writing from students, the only sure way to achieve this is to encourage them to notice things for themselves rather than to regurgitate bits of knowledge previously downloaded from the teacher, or the teacher's handouts.

I have argued that one approach which enlivens the experience of teaching Shakespeare is theatre and the realm, parallel to but not always dependent on text, of performance. The second approach which I believe to be essential to genuine engagement with Shakespeare is this process of poring over text, testing interpretations and finding new connections: a process requiring time and space, which somehow needs to be found even in the new A-level structures. (It is the kind of sustained scrutiny, moreover, which is not a part of the university teaching of Shakespeare – and a habit which therefore needs to be established if students are to continue with the subject in higher education.) Both approaches – the theatrical and the textual – have the advantage of emphasizing the life in Shakespeare's writing, the ever-shifting variety of dramatization and interpretation. Nor are they unrelated: a director of integrity should understand every line of a play on his or her own terms, and be certain that the actors do as well. (School productions of Shakespeare often suffer from a reluctance simply to cut lines which are not understood, or not spoken in a way that conveys understanding.)

But perhaps both these pillars – of close classroom engagement with Shakespeare's written language and of live, frequent in-school performance of his plays – are under threat. Listening to mandarins from organizations like the Qualifications and Curriculum Authority does not inspire me with confidence in the exams of the future. Will they maintain a prominent emphasis on Shakespeare's language, or be guided towards 'higher' critical or cultural approaches? Could modular structures expand to the extent of American semester-style evaluation?

Many of the features I have outlined which enable Shakespeare to survive and thrive as an entertainer alongside his status as a set author – the profusion of plays, the existence of boy-run magazines and websites which review theatre and the arts, the opportunities for creative writing, even School rituals like essay and declamation competitions – are precisely the kind which become harder to maintain alongside a proliferating public examination system. Eton has no aversion to examinations – quite the reverse: it has a rigorous tradition of biannual internal 'Trials'. But internal examinations at least have the advantage of being positioned at times which do not interfere with the broader cultural life of the School. Like many schools, Eton attempts to juggle the increasing burdens of public examination with its extra-curricular interests in a way that hinders neither.

My hope is that the very healthy culture of extra-curricular theatre, which has burgeoned alongside and complemented Eton's comparatively recent English and Drama Departments, will continue to ensure Shakespeare thrives here. Equally, I hope that those with a responsibility for devising and implementing examinations do not lead us away from close engagement with the text, towards the phoney citadels of cultural, contextual and critical abstraction.

Bibliography

Card, T., *Eton Renewed: A History of Eton College from 1860 to the Present Day* (John Murray, London, 1993).

Card, T., *Eton Established: A History from 1440 to 1860* (John Murray, London, 2001).

Eaglestone, R., *Doing English: A Guide for Literature Students* (Routledge, London, 2000).

Graham-Campbell, A., *The Rage for the Drama: Nineteenth Century Theatricals at Eton* (Eton College Library Archive, 1996).

Lyttelton, G. and Hart-Davis, R., *The Lyttelton Hart-Davis Letters*, ed. R. Hart-Davis (John Murray, London, 1978).

Meredith, M., *Five Hundred Years of Eton Theatre* (Tadberry Evedale, London, 2001).

Osborne, R., *Till I End My Song: English Music and Musicians 1440–1940, a Perspective from Eton* (The Cygnet Press, London, 2002).

CHAPTER 5

Shakespeare at 16–19

Sean McEvoy

In September 2001 nearly 250 young people aged between 16 and 19 embarked upon academic courses in English Literature or English at Varndean College. The study of a Shakespeare play was a central experience for the vast majority of these students. Varndean is a state sixth-form college in the northern suburbs of the newly enchartered city of Brighton and Hove. About a thousand young people come to us post-GCSE to study; most take A-level courses, but a significant number take vocational courses (ACVEs) at both Advanced and Intermediate Level. Of the 250 students studying English Literature and English in September 2001, about 120 were beginning the AS course in Literature, about 80 the A2, and some 50 were resitting the GCSE in English and thus completing a piece of Shakespeare coursework. The first years studied *The Merchant of Venice* or *Othello* for a term; the second years *King Lear* or *The Tempest*. Some second years studied Ben Jonson's *Volpone* instead of Shakespeare. Since Shakespeare at GCSE has been discussed elsewhere in this volume, my focus in this chapter will be upon English Literature at A-level, and in particular on the exciting times through which we are living as a result of the introduction of the new 'Curriculum 2000' specifications (syllabuses) introduced in England, Wales and Northern Ireland from September 2000.

Brighton is not a typical British seaside town (or city). It is not in fact a typical British town at all. The words 'liberal' and 'cosmopolitan' come too lazily to mind when describing the cultural background from which our students emerge – but that is only part of the picture. For many of them, Brighton's significance as a centre of 'club' culture, with all that that entails, is important. They have also grown up in a town whose large openly gay community is not just 'tolerated', but, I would say, is simply part of Brighton. Innovative media and information technology companies are important to the local economy. There are two universities; the radical reputation of the more senior of the two is not entirely dimmed. Thousands of foreign language students fill the streets in the summer months. Yet Brighton is still in very many ways a working-class town, even if working-class students constitute only a small minority in A-level English Literature classes. There are also many pockets of poverty and deprivation, particularly on the two large estates located to the north and east. Thousands of Brighton people commute to London every day.

The six Brighton secondary schools do not have sixth forms. After GCSE, students come either to us, to the other sixth-form college in Hove, or to the further education college. We do take about ten per cent of our students from the towns north of the South Downs and along the coast to the east, but the vast majority of the intake are students whose environment seems to make them receptive to the liberal arts and to liberal (and even radical) ideas. English Literature, History and Art are jointly the three most popular subjects at A-level in the College, with Psychology very close behind. Media Studies and Sociology recruit large numbers as well. Drama at the College enjoys a very high reputation locally and is always oversubscribed (as is the College as a whole). There are five teachers of A-level Literature in an English faculty which also includes

Media, Film, Drama, Music and Classical Civilization. All teach at least one other subject (usually English Language). They have a wide range of critical interests, but it would be fair to say that their approach to literature is broadly feminist and/or socialist in sympathy.

'Traditional' versus 'Modern'?

I mention this because I think it is important to the context of where Shakespeare studies stand at A-level today. The introduction by the government's QCA (Qualifications and Curriculum Authority) of the new specifications for English Literature from September 2000 has, I believe, caused what was a fault-line between two different approaches to the subject to become something of a chasm; and what separates the two camps is, in essence, political.

The examination performance of all students is now measured against five standard Assessment Objectives (AOs). Two of these objectives in particular have caused controversy, and in some cases, consternation among A-level teachers:

AO4   Candidates should be able to articulate independent opinions and judgements, informed by different interpretations of literary texts by other readers.

AO5i (AS Level, i.e. year one)   Candidates should be able to show understanding of the contexts in which literary texts are written and understood.

AO5ii (A2 Level, i.e. year two)   Candidates should be able to evaluate the significance of cultural, historical and other contextual influences on literary texts and study.

The import of AO4 would seem to be that students would need to be aware of what critics had written about the texts being studied in class; or, at the very least, show that they had considered a variety of views as expressed in class discussion. For many teachers this notion of views being 'informed by different interpretations of literary texts' seems to introduce an unwanted mediation in what they take to be the crucial relationship in the English classroom: that between the individual student and the text. For teachers whose training and outlook have placed 'personal response' at the centre of their practice, this objective might seem to require students to parrot and comment on critics rather than to respond to the text itself. Some even feel it could be a reversion to the kind of English done in the distant days before F. R. Leavis.

The fifth assessment objective has caused even more anxiety, as can be seen from the way that publishers rushed out a torrent of books in 2000–1 aimed at A-level Literature students and teachers with titles containing the word 'context'. The fear here is that teachers would be required to spend precious time in an already crowded course teaching large amounts of 'background' which they felt was of limited importance to their students' study of the text itself. Thus, instead of the traditional rapid canter through Shakespeare's biography followed by the showing of the opening of Laurence Olivier's film of *Henry V* in order to illustrate the Globe theatre, they would have to provide all sorts of social, cultural and historical information of an open-ended nature; information which they felt their students would find hard to deploy usefully in their studies. As an illustration of this attitude, when one of the four examining boards, OCR (Oxford, Cambridge and Royal Society of Arts), set its first Shakespeare paper in January 2001, one of the essay questions on *Othello* was in fact regarded by some teachers as both unfair and irrelevant:

How important do you think Venice is to the play *Othello*?

In your answer you should:

- set out clearly what you think Venice – the city and what it stands for – adds to the play;
- explain your views on Othello's relationship with Venice;
- comment on the place of relevant issues such as attitudes to outsiders.

The study of Shakespeare for many teachers remains the study of character, plot and theme. For them, the reason why Shakespeare holds his central place in the canon is because his plays have a universal, *timeless* greatness and relevance. The historical context (or 'background' as it is often revealingly called) is therefore always secondary to the plays themselves. They echo the line in Shakespeare's praise at which I am sure the ghost of Ben Jonson still shudders in regret, 'He was not of an age, but for all time'.[1]

That division, between those teachers who welcome the new requirement to teach Shakespeare's plays in the cultural, historical and theatrical contexts in which they were produced and are now received, and those who do not, is illustrated by two different specifications produced by the same examination body. The list of suggested coursework tasks for the examination of Shakespeare at AS-level in one of these specifications, AQA (Assessment and Qualification Alliance) 'B', produced by the old Northern Examinations and Assessment Board, includes these tasks (p. 25):

- a study of the performance history/reception of the text(s)
- comparison of different production(s) seen by the candidate

- detailed study of how the text was established
- detailed study of the text(s) in relation to audience (16th/17th century and contemporary)

But the other AQA specification, AQA 'A', the successor to the old personal-response dominated AEB 660 syllabus, might be seen to be dismissive in its attitude to contexts in its published teacher support material. The only suggested reading (p. 74) apart from websites offered in its Teachers' Guide is the old eight-volume *Pelican Guide to English Literature* edited by Boris Ford, first published between 1954 and 1961. Even though the series was revised as recently as 1983, these volumes nevertheless represent the criticism of the age before the advent of what has become known as 'literary theory'. AQA 'B' by comparison lists eight books in its Teachers' Guide (p. 41), at least six of which have a commitment to theory.

This is the crux of the matter. The tides of structuralist and post-structuralist criticism may well have partially receded from the university study of English, but what the 'theory' revolution has established firmly is the necessity of reading texts *inside* history, and not in some idealized nowhere-place. This means that we read texts as products both of their time and place, and within a discourse which has been created by the historical circumstances in which we find ourselves now. QCA's introduction of Assessment Objectives Four and Five can thus be seen as the bringing up-to-date of English Literature A-level: as the dissemination of the accepted ideas at the highest levels of study into schools and colleges. As Robert Eaglestone has argued in an important and influential book, A-level English had become dominated by a world-view that was developed as a subject in the first half of the twentieth century. Among other things this turns potentially exciting literature into bland exam fodder . . . All this risks making English into a subject studied as a bland ritual, a 'heritage' subject.[2]

What other academic subject would teach an approach and indeed a content at A-level that was now almost entirely superseded in the universities?

At Varndean, our teaching has been conducted in the spirit of Assessment Objectives Four and Five for some time; we stand on the other side of the divide from the views which I have outlined above. We do not accept that there can be such a thing as unmediated contact between student and text; we do not believe that a response to a text can be made without the involvement of contextual factors. We think that in what might be called the 'traditional' approach a whole host of interpretations and contextual factors *are* in fact brought to the reading of the text, but remain unacknowledged and therefore unexamined. Students have been aware of Shakespeare and forced to study him by statute throughout their school careers. As a cultural icon and emblem of Englishness he has a presence for them in the world beyond the classroom. The kind of unspoken attitudes which students bring to Shakespeare at A-level tend to include a notion that they are reading 'the greatest author in the world' – although, when challenged, they cannot generally articulate what this might mean without falling back on the well-inculcated notion that his work contains 'universal' truths and wisdom, usually about 'human nature'.

Students are also aware that an ability to appreciate Shakespeare is a marker in our society of being educated and intelligent, an idea which curiously enough seems to go back as far as the Preface for the 1623 Folio written by Shake-speare's first editors, John Hemmings and Henry Condell: 'read him therefore, and again and again. And if then you do not like him, surely you are in some manifest danger not to understand him'.[3] If you don't like Shakespeare, it is because you aren't bright enough to understand him! Neither do students come to us naive of the critical tradition. The extraor-dinary tenacity of A. C. Bradley's 1904 opinion on 'the tragic flaw', widely held and known by students, is quite remark-able.[4] Characters, they also believe, should be 'credible'; there should also be some virtuous ones with whom they can identify. None of this obviously contextual opinion is produced by direct contact with the text, as a 'personal response'. It is all, obviously, open to question. At Varndean we approach the study of Shakespeare with a different set of contextual opinions; but we are open and explicit about them, and so they are able to be challenged.

Some teachers think that an approach influenced by literary theory, even the kind of historicism we practice, is too advanced for this age group. But our students are quite familiar with the ideas of genre, audience, representation and ideology from their Media Studies and Social Science lessons. Those also studying Drama will have some acquaintance with Brecht's and Boal's ideas about performance. Some teachers claim that there is not time to introduce the contextual material that students require; we cannot see that they are able to come to an adequate understanding of the text without it. What kind of understanding can a seventeen-year-old have of *Othello* without knowledge of Venice and the Turks, Moors, Machiavelli, the romance tradition, courtly love and so on? It is not as if it is possible to read the text without interpreting at the same time; all understanding involves interpretation. Love, race and gender are complex notions and were not understood in London in 1604 in the same way as they are in Brighton in 2003. There are not universal values in the plays, but historically specific ones. Once students are aware of this they gain a perspective which allows them to be critical of the way concepts like race and gender are used in a superficial and even sinister way in our own society.

A Professor of Literature at a Ruskin College conference complained some years ago that A-level English 'taught students to write about characters in texts as if they were their friends today'. This is exactly what we are trying to avoid. We see A-level English Literature as an intermediate step between school and university. Despite the fact that 80 per cent of our students do not go on to read English at university, we pay them all the respect of offering them a serious *contemporary* academic discipline. I think some teachers see A-level as the culmination of school English, and therefore not different in kind from it. In consequence I have occasionally seen the elegant but critically banal paragraph marked more highly than one which struggles successfully – but still struggles – to express complex and demanding ideas. We see the study of Literature at sixteen-plus as far more than an advanced test of competence in reading and writing.

Classroom Practice

The obvious fact that the plays are written for performance is a crucial context. This means that the classroom performance of at least part of the text is an essential part of the experience; it means that we prefer prepared classroom readings given with theatrical energy to sight readings, and certainly to silent reading! Videos and tapes are used as much as possible, but we always use them critically, and comparatively where possible. Classroom reading and performance is geared towards interpretation by working on different ways of reading or acting scenes or parts of scenes. When we see a production in the theatre we go prepared to focus on how particular nominated moments have been played.

Though some contextual information is taught or researched by students as part of the introduction to a play, the use of contextual material or critical opinion tends to be integrated into classroom work. For instance, activities on *Hamlet* have included:

1. Work on the religious and political context, to include early modern and medieval views on revenge, ghosts, the Reformation, Machiavelli, the *Homilies on Obedience*, etc.
2. Work on the genre conventions of revenge tragedy, by a comparison of the plots and settings of other plays.
3. Comparative study of the 'To be or not to be' soliloquy in the First Quarto[5] and Folio[6] versions, and of Hamlet and the Player King's account of the death of Priam (II.ii. 450–518) in contrast to its source in Marlowe's *Dido, Queen of Carthage*.[7]
4. A full classroom rehearsal of the scene which contains *The Murder of Gonzago* (III. ii), examining the implications of different ways of performing different moments.
5. A comparison of specific moments in different film productions of the play, using the 1993 BFI Shakespeare Cinema Study Video containing extracts from Kozintsev, Olivier, Richardson, and Zeffirelli.
6. Writing the soliloquy that Gertrude never gives, or one for Ophelia which is less rigid and conventional than that which begins 'O, what a noble mind is here o'erthrown.'
7. An examination of the role of Ophelia which does not attempt to make her character 'consistent' but emphasizes and examines its fractures and discontinuities.

8. An examination of the *political* impact of the cutting of Fortinbras, both in past productions and in performance today.
9. Looking at and discussing extracts from traditional criticism by A. C. Bradley and T. S. Eliot, and at modern extracts by Graham Holderness, Catherine Belsey, Marilyn French, Elaine Showalter, Kate Flint and Raman Selden.

Activities 1, 2, 3, 4, 5, 6 and 8 are in one way or another focused on historical, cultural and political factors; 4 and 9 are more concerned with interpretation. There is of course considerable overlap between the two in most of the activities anyway.

Students find the work challenging, but it is certainly not beyond them. Varndean does not have a particularly able intake compared to many sixth-form colleges nationally, but it is one of the very best in the country at producing 'value added': our students perform far better than their GCSE results would indicate that they should. In the last few years our 'raw' results in English Literature have been good, but our pass and retention rates have been considerably better than the national average. If what we were offering was too demanding for A-level, it would be the least academically able who would either leave or fail.

For the purpose of writing this chapter I collected the opinions of a number of students who had either left college in the last two years or had just completed their A-levels. My sample was not scientific, but what students picked out as important and interesting was our focus on context and interpretation. One wrote that

At school the main purpose of studying Shakespeare seemed to be exploring the plot, characters, and their motivations as people. The language was put across as a barrier, something to overcome rather than appreciate as part of the subject. I didn't choose to do English A-level because of the prospect of more Shakespeare. I felt that at Varndean the emphasis placed on setting the context was crucial to making the plays seem valuable, relevant things to be studying – not just a history lesson. The opportunity to explore and question debates about and in the text made it enjoyable. It wasn't just about remembering information.

A mature student who had last read Shakespeare at a Secondary Modern in the 1970s, where 'it felt dull and therefore I switched off' wrote that

> We looked at the plays through various mediums. By visiting the theatre, watching videos, listening to tapes, acting out certain scenes, discussing critics' views as well as our own opinions, the experience of analysing, interpreting and understanding the text immediately became enjoyable.

I was encouraged here to see that this student, whether consciously or not, lists 'understanding' as the third term in the list after 'analysing' and 'interpreting'. She does not imply, I note, as in the traditional model, that understanding comes first and interpretation *later*. She suggests that understanding (and enjoyment!) comes through the process of analysis and interpretation.

Adherents of the traditional approach have claimed that to privilege criticism and historical context is actually to impose a limiting framework on what can and cannot be discussed, and to replace an open, liberal environment with a closed and restricted one. Indeed, one of the difficult parts of teaching in this way is to ensure that the students do not feel that you have all the right answers. All the students who responded, including the two quoted above, clearly enjoyed the opportunity to develop their *own* opinions in an academically rigorous way ('We were encouraged as a class to have varying viewpoints about what a play was about,' according to one student). I would also like to quote another ex-student, who is now reading English Literature at one of the new universities, to defend *us* from the suspicion of primarily being more concerned with politics than Shakespeare – and as, perhaps, a demonstration of how the focus on interpretation and context *can* be taken too far at the expense of the text, at least according to him!

> So far I've studied *Macbeth* at university. Very little knowledge of the play was required as we only seem to study literary criticism! This is really boring and I much preferred English at college. At college we spent quite a lot of time on each play/text, which was good as we could develop a quite detailed understanding. This doesn't happen at university. There aren't the same classroom discussions or acting out parts of scenes and so the plot and characters of the play seem to become irrelevant – which I think is totally wrong. Instead we just learn about these bitter feminist critics, or Marxists who just use the play as a tool to push forward their own agendas and beliefs.

Attitudes to Shakespeare

The political debate about Shakespeare's place in the curriculum seems to have lost its heat compared to the situation fifteen years ago. Ministers in the last Conservative government sought to claim the plays both as iconic validations of 'traditional' values and as invocations of a notion of 'Englishness' in the face of what were seen as two dangers: the threats of the break-up of Great Britain through Scottish and Welsh devolution on the one hand, and of closer political and economic integration with mainland Europe on the other. Not only did they make Shakespeare examinations compulsory in both phases of secondary education, but their public pronouncements asserted again and again that 'Shakespeare was a Tory'. In response, opponents of the government in the universities wrote perceptively of the way that, when it came to Shakespeare, study guides, classroom methods and the examination system were often complicit in the inculcation of Conservative values. In the broader field of national culture, both 'high' and 'popular', the same phenomenon was analysed and subjected to critique. At a 1993 conference on 'Shakespeare in Education' Professor Richard Wilson commented on the 1983 pronouncements of Chancellor Nigel Lawson, who had suggested

> that because 'Shakespeare was a Tory', who wrote 'from a Tory point of view', Tory values were universal too, and the syllogism provided the classic instance of what Pierre Bourdieu has described as the 'symbolic violence' of pedagogic action: the circular logic 'whereby power relations are perceived not for what they objectively are, but in a form that renders them legitimate in the eyes of the beholder'.[8]

The validity of much of this analysis still stands; indeed, one of the reasons why some teachers take what I have called a 'modern', historicizing approach to the plays in the classroom stems from a political opposition to what they take to be the so-called 'universal' values and ideas implicated in the 'traditional' approach.

The political ground has, however, obviously shifted since the 1980s. The Labour government has made no such political claims for Shakespeare as a cultural and educational force. Indeed, they could be seen to be quietly dismantling Shakespeare's central status in the English curriculum. Only one play is now required at A-level rather than two (I have chosen to teach my second years Ben Jonson's *Volpone* rather than *King Lear* or *The Tempest*, but only because I love that comedy so much). The new Assessment Objectives have at least partially undermined the notion of a universal genius existing outside history (hence, their controversial nature). The GCSE in English Language first examined in 2003 will not require the study of any Shakespeare, thus abandoning the notion, explicit in the syllabuses produced during the Thatcher/Major years, that the study of Shakespeare's English would be a means of improving the written and spoken English of young people in the twenty-first century.[9]

It also became much harder to see Shakespeare as a wellspring of pure Englishness and traditional values in the wake of Hollywood's rediscovery of the bard in the 1990s. Baz Luhrmann's 1996 *William Shakespeare's Romeo and Juliet* and John Madden's *Shakespeare in Love* (1998) presented Shakespeare as anything but imbued with traditional values. Both were very successful at the box office. In the first, Shakespeare's text is fused with the pop video and action movie in a witty, high-energy and innovative film which is still extraordinary close to the spirit of the whole text. The second is a romantic comedy where an adulterous and rather cowardly Shakespeare is no better than he should be, and where a woman plays a far more dominant role than any would have done in the early modern theatre. Young people saw in the films what many academics claim today. First, they saw that in our globalized culture Shakespeare is no longer just an *English* figure but is now, perhaps, a world literary figure who belongs to all. Second, they saw that the texts of plays are not now a repository of ancient wisdom for the initiated, but the basis of a new generation of mass entertainment products, amongst other things. In this new political and cultural environment, students are perhaps less aware of Shakespeare's iconic central status in the English canon than they were.

Here is a pair of contrasting statements from two Varndean English Literature students at the end of their course. They were both asked whether they felt that Shakespeare should be a compulsory text at A-level:

> I do agree that every student should study Shakespeare, although I know that the majority of students would struggle at some point. I think that every English student should be proud of an English writer known worldwide. It is fascinating for a student to study the language in the plays as we can see how language changes over time. Shakespeare's plays also mix all literature elements of prose, verse and acting into one so a lot can be learned from Shakespeare. His plays are seen as great literature as they have so many contemporary issues which we can learn from the 'strangest' Shakespeare plays.

> I fail to see why the examining body feels that Shakespeare is a particularly necessary or relevant topic for all A-level students to study. I feel that if literature from this particular period is a very important subject, a range of writers should be offered for study, as opposed to one.

All the students I asked came down on one side of the debate or the other, with a majority for the first position. The power of society's conventional ideas about Shakespeare's 'greatness' was still evident in many answers. Several retentionist students mentioned 'contemporary relevance', but others said things like 'It sets you in good stead academically and socially', or 'Enjoying it made me feel grown up' or that 'Shakespeare is an important part of our literary history, so I think everyone should experience studying it. That's not to say that everyone should like it, they should just form an opinion of it.' Although the abolitionists had all enjoyed Shakespeare, they thought that someone should at least 'go to great lengths to explain to your normal A-level student why he [Shakespeare] is so important, not just take it for granted that we know', or that teachers should have 'the power to choose a more accessible alternative, according to their students' ability and even cultural background'.

Extremely prevalent in the students' responses was a feeling of pride that they had come through a kind of rite of passage. They had achieved an understanding of Shakespeare's language, which had been for many a barrier that they had ducked under rather than hurdled at GCSE. Many of these students had also studied Donne, Milton and Jonson at A-level, or tackled challenging contemporary authors like Toni Morrison or Howard Barker. I am sure that the ability to understand Shakespeare in particular retains its social and intellectual kudos. One wrote that 'There was a sense that Shakespeare was a more "serious" subject, and so I initially approached it with more of a fear of being wrong than other texts.' I feel it also remains a powerful marker of class distinction – an uneasiness about this was evident, if not explicit, in several student responses, for example: 'A-level English Literature is synonymous with Shakespeare and if a student has experienced poor teaching at secondary level they would find it intimidating.'

Our students in general arrive worried about the language,

it would seem, and leave having enjoyed the plays as *plays*, and with some sense of achievement. Those who go on to take English in some form in higher education – and about one in five do so – seem to be well prepared. An anecdote to this effect from a student who went on to Royal Holloway College, London demonstrates this – but it might also point out that the kind of literary study we do at Varndean is not typical:

> During the 'Shakespeare' course at my first year at university we would discuss the text in a group with a lecturer, just as at A-level. I would simply repeat the same points and attitude learnt at A-level, but they were largely different to the rest of the group. The lecturer came up to me afterwards and congratulated my 'good points', but they weren't anything I'd learnt at university. The lecturer seemed surprised.

My own feeling is that after centuries of explicit promotion as England's own timeless genius, Shakespeare remains high-status cultural capital, for good or ill. It is the duty of a democratic state education system to make access to this capital as widespread as possible. In particular, we should be making it possible for our students to make their own readings, to appropriate the plays – especially if the readings they make from socially or politically disadvantaged positions challenge the political assumptions that have given the texts their high cultural status to start with. Let me stress that this is not an argument for teaching students to understand Shakespeare so that they can condemn it. All early modern literature is hard for modern seventeen- and eighteen-year-olds to understand, but Shakespeare's language is not yet so distant from ours that the sheer quality of his plays as drama, poetry, and thought will not move and excite a class if they are taught properly. But so will Donne's *Songs and Sonnets*, and so will Jonson's *The Alchemist* and *Volpone*, and so will much else from this period. Both the continuing cultural status and the excellence of his work will ensure that Shakespeare's place remains secure at A-level, I think. But we must be prepared, in future, to keep open the debate with our students about why it should be taught.

In Performance

I am not however so sanguine about the future of student productions of Shakespeare at sixth-form level. In my experience at least the new curriculum, and other developments, have made it very unlikely that the tradition of school and college productions of Shakespeare will survive.

During the 1990s there was a regular programme of productions of all kinds at Varndean which were not part of the examination courses in Theatre Studies. They were directed not only by drama teachers, but also by other members of staff who had an interest in the theatre. Rehearsals took place outside of college hours. *The Comedy of Errors*, *The Tempest*, *Hamlet*, *Measure for Measure* and *Othello* were produced, but also Jonson's *Volpone*, Marlowe's *The Jew of Malta*, Shakespeare and Fletcher's *The Two Noble Kinsmen*, Middleton's (or Tourneur's?) *The Revenger's Tragedy* and Heywood's (some would say deservedly!) neglected *The Wise Woman of Hogsden*. Casting was usually by open audition, and thus many of the actors, although not all, tended to be those already taking A-level Theatre Studies. Those participating in these productions gained an insight into the plays which can be achieved by no other means. They had to master the rhetorical and logical patterns of the language and the skill of blank verse speaking; they ingested the vital importance of pace, energy and timing in the realization of these works of art, a crucial dimension so often missing in classroom appreciation of the plays; they enacted the visual and gestural realization of the language and felt the audience response – without which the whole experience is lame. As a teacher directing many of these plays, I felt I learnt more about the workings of early modern drama than thousands of hours reading criticism and scholarship could provide. There were very many other benefits to these productions, but what we all learnt about Shakespeare was irreplaceable. Some English and Theatre Studies students would leave having studied three plays and performed in a further two in the space of their two years at college. Each production represented at least three months' work, with students – especially those in the lead roles – contributing a great deal of their time and energy.

Two principal factors have ended this tradition, at least for the moment. The new AS and A2 Drama (and the Edexcel Drama A-level before them) have a much larger element of assessed practical work than the old Theatre Studies A-level. Numbers on these courses have increased rapidly, and we have also introduced the vocational Performing Arts course. Rehearsal and performance space is in constant use to meet examination requirements, and the demands on drama staff have been enormous. Consequently there is not enough rehearsal or performance space or time any more. The second factor is one which I am sure other schools and colleges will recognize: students themselves have very little time for extra-curricular activities. First year A-level students now typically take four or even five subjects, and face public exams crucial for university entrance after only nine months at college. There is also plenty of part-time work available in Brighton, and students not only want to acquire the means to take advantage of the town's social and cultural opportunities, but also strive to start saving money for their time at university. Even rehearsals for examination performances have to be negotiated around student work commitments.

The exam regulations about cast sizes and the necessarily short rehearsal periods have made Shakespeare a very unsuitable production choice for the new Drama AS and A2 courses. The last Shakespeare production at the college was in fact an exam performance for the old Drama syllabus, a brilliant production of *The Tempest* directed by one of the drama staff. She reversed the genders of the protagonists and set the play in a kind of futuristic age. The part of Ariel was shared between two actors, both of whom were accomplished dancers; there was a particularly tortured and intelligent Prospero; music was constant and integral. The text was edited and rearranged to make the first hour of the play achieve much more impact than it often has. It was a memorable end to a fine tradition.

Conclusion

A-level is the stage at which students really encounter Shakespeare's qualities as a dramatist and dramatic poet. I am confident that these qualities, together with the cultural status that mastery of his plays still bestows, will continue to maintain Shakespeare's central position in the curriculum at this level for some time, whatever the political implications of that centrality may be.

A newspaper article in the *Independent* (24 April 2001) pronounced Shakespeare's day to be over. The writer, Jonathan Myerson, had visited a Royal Shakespeare Company production of *Cymbeline* in London and found it mostly incomprehensible and therefore tedious. He claimed that the gap between modern and early modern English was becoming too vast. At some point Shakespeare's English will no doubt be as relatively inaccessible as Chaucer's, but I think that he is wrong about today. There are, however, a couple of messages here. Shakespeare must be taught (and directed and acted) with the energy, directness and lack of pretension that was characteristic of the early modern theatre; furthermore, we would be most unwise to ignore the historical and cultural distance between the early seventeenth-century London and the particular early twenty-first-century cultures in which the plays may be received. I suspect that in future the decline of the political totems and outlook with which Shakespeare was traditionally associated may undermine the plays' status as cultural icons. They will then only survive on their virtues as drama if we can contextualize them for each new generation. We should no longer pretend that they simply speak clearly to us across the centuries; that is the way to condemn them to students' apathy, and worse.

Notes

1. *The Oxford Authors: Ben Jonson*, ed. Ian Donaldson, p. 454 (Oxford University Press, 1985).
2. Robert Eaglestone, *Doing English* (first edition), p. 530 (Routledge, 2000).
3. *The Riverside Shakespeare*, (second edition), ed. G. Blakemore Evans, p. 95 (Houghton Mifflin, 1997).
4. A. C. Bradley, *Shakespearian Tragedy* (second edition), p. 34 (Macmillan, 1904).
5. *The First Quarto of Hamlet*, K. O. Irace (ed.) (Cambridge University Press, 1998).
6. 3.1, lines 55–89 (*The Riverside Shakespeare*).
7. C. Marlowe, *Dido, Queen of Carthage* and *The Massacre at Paris*, ed. H. J. Oliver (Methuen, 1968).
8. 'NATO's pharmacy: Shakespeare by prescription', in John J. Joughin (ed.), *Shakespeare and National Culture*, pp. 58–80 (Manchester University Press, 1997).
9. Compared to the media uproar about Shakespeare in the

1980s there was, interestingly, little news coverage of this development. Having been nominated by the National Association for the Teaching of English to discuss the issue on BBC radio, my interview was withdrawn from the running order at the last moment and replaced by a report on the new manager of Luton Town Football Club.

CHAPTER 6

Teaching Shakespeare in Higher Education

Tiffany Stern

I work at Oxford Brookes University with students from a wide variety of backgrounds: there are teenagers and 60-year-old mothers, well-read and scarcely-read, native and non-native English speakers. Not all of them are studying English exclusively: about half are taking joint honours, generally combining English with History, Publishing or a Modern Language. They are also mostly women, a strange imbalance characteristic of the subject of English in higher education, at least in the UK. As a result of the mixture, no shared background of knowledge can be assumed. Some students have studied a Shakespeare play at school; many have never read him in a scholarly way before. Somehow all of these different people have to be catered for.

At the same time, undergraduates at university now do not have the indifference of their predecessors (the undergraduates of fifteen years ago who had generally had little or no enjoyable exposure to Renaissance drama). Films like Kenneth Branagh's *Much Ado About Nothing* and *Henry V*, and Baz Luhrmann's *Romeo and Juliet* have put Shakespeare back into the world he came from – the world not of 'literature' or 'education', but entertainment. His plays, slick and sparkling on the screen, are now thought to have contemporary relevance

because they have contemporary *cachet*. Added to that, Tom
Stoppard's *Shakespeare in Love* has supplemented the
mystique of the plays with the mystique of the writer. Now
Shakespeare the man is no longer a half-bald engraving, but a
handsome sufferer of Freudian Angst: 'the bard' finally has
understandable twentieth-century values. Yet Stoppard's film
also illustrates how, as an icon, Shakespeare can be entirely
separated from his words. In marketing, 'Shakespeare' is often
simply his head – on the 'will power' badge, the slipper, the
mug, and smiling a Mona Lisa smile out from a bankcard.
Alternatively, he is the sound-bite on 'Out damn'd spot!'
erasers and 'I do very well note it' telephone pads, making
fragments of Shakespeare into self-contained wholes that live
outside their texts, and well out of context: the Shakespeare
industry does not necessarily need any actual Shakespeare at
all to sustain itself. For contemporary students, then, Shakespeare has quite a different feel from the previous generation's
Shakespeare. They may know a line without having a sense of
where it comes from, they may know some bored journalist's
conspiracy theories about authorship; at the same time they
may also know a play in its screen-version almost off by heart.
Certainly, as Shakespeare is differently handled by the marketing industry from his fellow dramatists, students will have a
sense of him that they do not have of other playwrights. But
what will that sense be? Probably that Shakespeare is likeable,
jokey, slightly kitsch, but also stylish – and performed by
people they would like to sleep with. This means that undergraduates these days want to study 'Shakespeare' partly
because of the strange and misguided ideas they have about
what a Shakespeare play – and what 'Shakespeare' – is.

The cinema in some ways adds to the problem. Screen-play
familiarity with a Shakespeare text, in particular, is not the
same as knowing the actual play. True, undergraduates no

longer start university hampered with that 'churchy' reverence for Shakespeare ('Not fun, but *so* good for you') that more old-fashioned schools have sometimes foisted on their pupils. On the other hand, the cinema makes Shakespeare accessible by cutting out a lot of what he wrote: film is a visual medium. Branagh, for instance, excised difficult lines from *Much Ado About Nothing* and, not trusting the play's words to produce the desired level of humour, fiddled with deckchairs, substituting physical jokes for text to ensure the audience would keep laughing. Students, coming from this to undoctored Shakespeare presented, as it so often is, weighed down with footnotes in great and serious tomes, can feel as though they have been cheated, let down: the reality of the text can disappoint rather than thrill them. It is the job of the lecturer to stop that happening; to find a balance between the historical writer and the media-icon. It is, therefore, helpful to take what the student comes to a class with (that is why clips from films are so vital), and then put it inside a much broader context.

At Oxford Brookes Shakespeare is taught as an 'option', only offered to students who have completed a core course on 'The Renaissance' (which consists of twelve texts, including *King Lear*). This means that only second- and third-year undergraduates can take the Shakespeare paper – although all first years read *Othello* as part of their 'Texts, Problems, and Approaches' introductory critical course, in which *Othello* is more or less a gloss on Alan Sinfield's 'Cultural Materialism, *Othello*, and the Politics of Plausibility'.[1] That first-year moment can leave them confused – *Othello's* tragedy becomes the fact that Othello and Desdemona do not fit in with prevailing ideologies of race or gender. My Shakespeare option course, which puts Shakespeare in a less politicized historical framework, aims to give the students a different kind of approach. It is, as I will later suggest, the kind of course that is now starting to be found in universities as a response to, and an extension of, new historicism and cultural materialism.

As the study of Shakespeare at Brookes is confined to the undergraduates who already have a Renaissance background, the plays can be looked at with an understanding of historical context underlying what is read. But the negative outcome of this is that not all students will take the Shakespeare course: it is possible to graduate with an English degree without ever having studied England's most famous playwright. This is partly connected to a larger problem that Brookes, with every other university, now faces. The days when English degrees were given for close New Critical readings of 'canonical' texts are passed. Now degrees must offset canonical texts (having, of course, emphasized that a canon does not exist) with alternative literatures, as well as critical theory. Yet the new courses must, as ever, all fit within three years' space – meaning that something, or someone, has to go. What is happening is that authors who were once thought the foundation of English Literature are being edged aside, as indeed is the term 'English Literature', with 'English' giving way to 'Englishes' or 'Comparative' or 'Cultural', and 'Literature' to 'Studies'. Shakespeare sometimes loses out as a result (a couple of years ago there were discussions about dropping the separate Shakespeare paper from the Cambridge University Tripos); he is punished for being mainstream and famous, a repository for the 'bad' values of earlier generations of scholars.

If not every student studies the Shakespeare option, being able to teach Shakespeare clearly inside his period is a great consolation. And the historical approach to literature does seem to be becoming more and more prevalent in universities. English literature, which remoulded itself first around linguistics, then around philosophy, now appears to be looking towards history for its new direction. In Brookes, a sense of what humanism is, what the Reformation was, and the anxieties surrounding monarchical succession in the early seventeenth century is not only desirable, it is expected. So Shakespeare is prevented from becoming 'other' – a timeless genius working outside any knowable system of values (that is how students who have studied Shakespeare at school have often received him). Rooted inside a known period, contemporary allusions spring to life without the need for those ponderous footnotes. Undergraduates are expected to have an idea of why so many plays have an obsession with asking whether 'wrong' people are taking the throne; to feel the novelty and irony underlying the words 'Britain' and 'British' (reintroduced by King James in 1603) in the title *Cymbeline, King of Britain* and in the *Lear* tag 'Fee, fie, foe, fum, I smell the blood of a British man'. Fortunately, history, and Renaissance history in particular, is popular not only inside the undergraduate worlds of literature and history; but is also generally modish, at least for the present. Coffee-table books and television series are plundering history for its stories much as Shakespeare did; even if students have not read much on the early modern period, they can be expected to have at least a TV versing in it.

My 'Revenge in the Shakespearean Playhouse' is a text-in-context course, that at first I thought was unique and individual. Looking at it, however, I realize that it is part of a movement to expand Shakespeare studies beyond the author and into the playhouse and printing-house. The movement is possibly more prevalent in the USA than here at present, for reasons I will examine, after explaining the nature of the course itself.

'Revenge in the Shakespearean Playhouse' explores revenge in early modern drama, comparing Shakespeare's plays with others written at roughly the same time, and

looking at the way different writers deal with the same
dramatic theme. It aims to give students not just Shakespeare
but Shakespeare inside his world; therefore, a sense of the
connections with works written by different playwrights who
shared the same historical and intellectual contexts is considered very important, providing an intellectual focus that
automatically suggests ways of evaluating, criticizing or
approaching Shakespeare. *Hamlet* is linked to Kyd's *The
Spanish Tragedy* in showing how Shakespeare's play can be
seen as a sophistication – and in some senses a parody – of
the revenge tragedy type; *Coriolanus* is added to give another
variation on the revenge-play theme (*Coriolanus* being a
revenge-play against a city). The course is further loosely
divided into 'Men and Revenge' (Kyd, *The Spanish Tragedy*,
Cyril Tourneur, *The Revenger's Tragedy*, Shakespeare,
Hamlet, Shakespeare, *Coriolanus*) and 'Women and Revenge'
(Shakespeare, *Macbeth*, Webster, *The White Devil*, Thomas
Middleton, *The Changeling*, Shakespeare, *Cymbeline*). This
division is a response to the fact that such a large number of
women attend the course, many of whom instinctively take a
feminist slant on the literature they read (feminism is also
strongly stressed on several of the other courses they study).
Renaissance tragedies are rich and complex in their approach
to women and to ideas of femininity ('masculine' women and
'effeminate' men, 'chaste' women and 'luxurious' men, 'mad'
women and 'mad' men); they therefore provide an excellent
starting point for the exploration of the construction of
gender in the early modern period. Not only that, but early
modern tragedies have long appealed to feminist critics, and
powerful works of modern criticism, often written by
women, give challenging models of literary and historical
interpretation for the students to work from – ranging from
Germaine Greer's classic *The Female Eunuch* (1970)[2], to

Dympna Callaghan's *A Feminist Companion to Shakespeare* (2000).[3]

The title 'Revenge in the Shakespearean Playhouse' indicates another important theme in the course: the theatre. Shakespeare's writing is put inside the conditions that shaped it; plays are examined as they circulated and as they appeared as drama and texts, with playhouse circumstances mediating textual transformations. Each week is dedicated to different kinds of historical/theatrical contexts for the drama in order to build up a sense of how the early modern theatre affected the writing and presentation of plays. Students are made aware of the physical nature of the stage world for which the plays were written; they are taught about the thrust stage, its roof painted with pictures of stars (the 'heavens'), and its under-stage ('hell'). This enables them to envision the stage space as a metaphorical sandwich and to use this to 'read' entrances or exits from hell and heaven and understand what they might mean. The ghost of old Hamlet, for instance, goes down to 'the cellerage' under the stage, from where he cries out; what should the audience conclude from that, while Hamlet wonders whether he has seen his father or 'a goblin damned'? Similarly, where does Hamlet gesture to when he talks of the 'heavens fretted with golden fire', and how would the audience have understood him? Does he motion out to 'our' heaven, or inward into his own (and how do such meta-theatrical references relate to the play-within-the-play, the antic disposition, and the whole scheme of 'playing' inside *Hamlet*)? There are a number of useful, student-friendly books and websites on Shakespeare in the theatre. Andrew Gurr, in particular, has written fascinatingly on the nature of the playhouse and its relation to the text, in his books *Playgoing in Shakespeare's London*, and *The Shakespearean Stage*).[4]

The course is taught by lecture and seminar; the seminar is closely text-based, the lecture much broader in its remit, providing the historical background and some of the parameters for later discussion. There are eight weeks of teaching, and so eight lectures: (1) early modern history and the rise of the playhouse; (2) early modern writing: dramatists' plays and actors' parts; (3) early modern religion: censorship and textual revision; (4) early modern education: rhetoric, poetry and action; (5) early modern attitudes to kingship: rehearsal and 'he who plays the king . . .'; (6) early modern printing: texts from stage to print house; (7) early modern xenophobia: theatrical notions of 'abroad'; (8) early modern music: songs, props and plays. Lectures include snippets of films, references to other plays performed in Shakespeare's time but not specifically covered in the course, illustrations from the period in reproduction, and photographs from modern productions. In this way an attempt is made to bridge the gap between performance 'then' and 'now'. Particularly helpful is the opening of Kenneth Branagh's *Henry V* in which the 'O for a muse of fire' prologue is spoken against images of cameras in a film-studio: the modes of production are very different, but questions – about imagination and artifice, fact and fiction, playing and 'playing' – are the same.

I teach less Shakespeare in 'Revenge in the Shakespearean Playhouse' than in the course it replaces. It might at one level seem strange to have Shakespeare classes not totally given over to Shakespeare. But Shakespeare's elevation over the past four centuries to a position of pre-eminent singularity by no means mirrors his position in his own time (a period much less author-obsessed, in which many plays were written collaboratively). Shakespeare-in-context courses at many universities are designed in this way, including as context not just London, the theatre, etc., but also non-Shakespearian plays (Shakespeare being equally, of course, context to Middleton and Webster). Incidentally, 'context', like 'text', is a laden new historicist word.

The Brookes Shakespeare option is assessed by essays: one mid-term and another at the end of term. The essay questions, together with a reading list, are given to students in the first week, but they are designed to pick up on the themes explored over the eight-week course: there are some on the playhouse ('How has scholarship on the Elizabethan playhouse changed our understanding of any two plays?'); some on other texts ('Write about the relationship of imitation and parody between Shakespeare and his contemporaries'); some on the treatment of revenge ('Is there a difference between the treat-ment of male revengers and female revengers in any two or more early modern tragedies?'); some on the treatment of women ('Is sexuality in any two or more plays seen as a force for good or for evil?'); and some on the issue of textual in-determinacy ('Does knowing more about a text affect your reading of it?'). Students also have the opportunity to design questions of their own.

My course is very different from the 'Power and Politics in Shakespeare' that was in place when I arrived. But both the 'Power' and 'Revenge' courses are traceable to ways of looking at Shakespeare that became modish in the 1980s, each reflect-ing what are at root 1980s' sets of values, but each following a different trajectory. The 1980s, as I see it, mark the last time absolutely new ways of thinking about Shakespeare were articulated; courses in most universities can be traced to deci-sions made in that decade. Without delving into the complex history of the rise and application of critical theory to English literature in general, which has an older heritage, I should perhaps simply give what I take to be a summary of what happened to critical theory with respect to Shakespeare in order to explain what was behind 'Power and Politics' – and where 'Revenge' came from.

From the 1960s onwards, when it was decided that New Criticism was beset with problems – specifically that it deemed as 'literature' only texts that conformed in various ways to certain old boys' agendas (which it then dehistoricized and fetishised) – a number of critical theories were applied to give literature a more political context, including feminism, Marxism, and structuralism. For a while, these different approaches floated generally about within literature, without being universally embraced, or particularly applied to Shakespeare. But in the 1980s a series of articles and two important books changed all that. Rather than applying theory that had its roots elsewhere to Shakespeare, buttoning philosophical cast-offs onto a body they do not remotely fit, these new theories were articulated in books that were *about* Shakespeare and the Renaissance: they were theories that arose directly out of Shakespeare studies, and their textbooks were themselves also works of Shakespeare criticism. Naturally, they changed the world of Shakespeare courses. One of these books was Jonathan Dollimore's *Radical Tragedy: Religion, Ideology and Power in the Drama of Shakespeare and his Contemporaries*,[5] and the other was Stephen Greenblatt's *Shakespearean Negotiations: The Circulation of Social Energy in Renaissance England*[6] (it followed on from *Renaissance Self-Fashioning*,[7] which had itself reshaped Renaissance studies). Each explored how Shakespeare's works were shaped by context, but rather than looking simply at historical context they looked at the social and cultural constructs that make up historical context. They argued that the material circumstances surrounding a literary text are, in fact, also texts ('text', like 'context', was a word freely embraced at that time, its Latin origin in 'net' and 'weaving' implying general interconnectedness), and argued against privileging Shakespeare's plays against other activities, every event being equally a 'text'. Both approaches were thus historical, but with a new angle on history. Both are often connected with Marxism: cultural materialism has, broadly, a particular interest in the underdog – women, the lower class, racial outsiders; new historicism has, broadly, its emphasis on the top of the social hierarchy – the church, the monarchy, the upper class.

'Power and Politics in Shakespeare', the course in place when I arrived at Brookes, was a descendant of the cultural materialist/new historicist movements. It was a lecture series with an 'agenda'. The students studied largely history (or historical) plays – *Julius Caesar*, *Anthony and Cleopatra*, *Richard II*, *1 and 2, Henry IV* and *Henry V* – with additions of *The Taming of the Shrew* (misogyny), and *The Tempest* (colonial outrages). This was a course about power-struggles, power-hierarchies and power-structures. It looked past Shakespeare to the political and social ideologies that formed his society and the societies he wrote about, and this had the effect of making his plays seem to be, collectively, subversive attempts to undermine the power structure and criticize authority. This was the strength and weakness of the option. My feeling about 'Power and Politics' was that it was punchy, exciting and provocative, but also angry: a course in which Shakespeare either presented a number of outmoded beliefs to be criticized against a series of values that he was not in a position to hold, or in which Shakespeare rightly lifted his weak voice against a perverted political society, but only in such a way that he could not quite be heard. A course of this nature does not give much time to the non-political aspects of a play: for instance, its language. The plays as plays are not particularly addressed; the plays are *about* political injustice.

The danger of lecture series of this kind (and they continue

to be popular) is that they explore certain fixed ideas to which
plays always in some way conform, either by actually conforming, or by not conforming, itself seen as telling. In this
way, the criticism is always confirmed by the plays, not because
of the nature of the plays, but because of the nature of the criticism: no text can be said to be simply outside the whole issue.
Shakespeare courses that are as heavily reliant as this on one
mode of criticism, moreover, can make critical texts as important as – and sometimes more important than – Shakespeare's
actual writing. Talking to 'Power and Politics' students, I felt
that they had not been given much of a chance to 'appreciate'
the plays through, for instance, close reading. Indeed, they had
not really addressed the plays non-politically at all. This meant
that they came away with a rather patronizing approach
towards Shakespeare and his world: he and his contemporaries
were 'primitive', living in a backwards England where social
injustice was the norm, and language, particularly poetry, was
resorted to by writers with ideas too potentially subversive to
be articulated in a 'normal' fashion. As for the plays themselves, the students looked for a 'purpose' for their being
written and, when they could not find one, were puzzled. I was
asked why, for instance, *Antony and Cleopatra* was tragic:
what was the 'reason' behind *Anthony and Cleopatra*?

Power and politics courses provided, in their time, a correc-
tive to the Shakespeare of the romantic characters and tragic
traits: the Edwardian Shakespeare who came straight out of
A. C. Bradley's *Shakespearean Tragedy* of 1904 and who was
still, bizarrely, flourishing in the universities of the 1970s. That
strictly moral Shakespeare made little sense against the preoccupations of that decade, and that he was repositioned in the
1980s was less of a surprise than the fact that it had taken so
long. The pervasive Bradley influence (recently restated in
Harold Bloom's *Shakespeare: The Invention of the Human*,[8]

which more or less claims that Shakespeare 'invented' personality) is slightly puzzling. True, Bradley was a marvellously thoughtful and insightful critic, and he provided, in his own day, an answer to the oracular Victorian style of Shakespeare criticism, replacing it with psychological criticism (he was writing in the Freudian age), and so analysing Shakespeare as an interpreter of the human soul. But he was very much concerned with the obsessions of his time (another stark example of how period-based criticism is). Desiring to make Shakespeare a 'classical' writer, he sought out in each of his tragic protagonists Aristotelian fatal flaws, despite knowing that the theory of Greek tragedy, as he himself put it, 'applies only imperfectly in the works of Shakespeare'; anxious to make Shakespeare conservatively Christian at heart, he imposed on him a view of tragedy where the tragic universe ultimately upholds a moral order. Though it took universities 70-odd years to abandon this style of criticism, Bradley continues to live on in the schoolroom – my own education was strictly Bradleian – so that much classroom teaching of Shakespeare is now 100 years behind current criticism. This is probably partly because Bradley wrote with a lucid, accessible prose style, and many modern critics do not: current criticism's failure to be approachable has limited its readership and, largely, confined it to university. Another reason is presumably that school-teachers and writers of school examination papers are often people who passed through university some time ago and have not updated their critical reading; school therefore reflects the university teaching of yesteryear. Bridging the critical gap between school Shakespeare and university Shakespeare is another task for the lecturer. The views that are hardest to get students to drop concern the tragic flaw that every protagonist is said to possess – 'jealousy' in the case of Othello, 'ambition' in the case of Macbeth. It helps to point out that Hamlet's flaw, usually described as 'indecision' or 'procrastination', is never obvious from reading the play (in which Hamlet *does* kill Claudius, only to discover, in the way of tragedy, that the man behind the arras was not the king at all but was, instead, the 'foolish fond' Polonius). That particular flaw was first 'noticed' by Samuel Taylor Coleridge, a poet famous for his inability to complete poems or anything else, who also remarked: 'I have a smack of Hamlet myself, if I may say so.'

Having brought about the updating of Bradley-style Shakespeare classes, I wonder whether such focused, driven, single-minded courses as 'Power and Politics' will continue much longer. The themes they raised are clearly important, but the socialist fervour that underwrote them can now itself be seen in historical context as a response to the Thatcher/Reagan world of the 1970s. If America is anything to go by, that has passed its peak, along with a number of other highly theorized methods of investigating Shakespeare (at its most extreme in King's College, Cambridge, where, for a while, students were taught only theory and expected to study the Shakespeare on their own). One reason for this is practical. There are now too many theories around for all to be taught, leaving the lecturer in the awkward position of either having to plump for one, or give a literature course that becomes a guide to theoretical approaches with no space for the actual texts. Another is simply the passage of time. Theoretical approaches in their starkest form came to England from America (though they were often Continental in origin). As with cinema films, we received them later and were just starting to be thrilled by the novelty when America was becoming bored by the familiarity. Now, in the USA, and increasingly here, theory is being softened and reduced to 'themes' rather than 'writers': *methods* of thinking about literature, rather than self-contained literary approaches. In his controversial book *Shakespeare After Theory*,[9] David Scott Kastan writes '[Theory's] day has passed, [and] we are in what theorists might term a post-theoretical moment', adding 'not because theory has been discredited [but] because its claims have proven so compelling and productive'. His feeling, writing in New York in the late 1990s, is that scholars are now teaching Shakespeare in a historical but theoretically sophisticated way, bringing to lectures an awareness of the author's agendas, and a sense of what the reader adds to the text. His preferred method straddles new historicism and new bibliography, and something of it can already be seen in numerous courses, my own 'Revenge' course included. When I reshaped Brookes' Shakespeare option, I took from New Historicism/Cultural Poetics an interest in the broader context that a play lived inside, and a sense of the complexities surrounding the 'underdog'. But I dropped a lot of the political vehemence, so that my context-based course, with its emphasis on the role of women in the Renaissance, can be traced to ideas raised by Marxist movements, but not to the movements themselves. It advocates understanding different schools of Shakespeare criticism, rather than subscribing to one.

The other heritage my course has clearly inherited from the 1980s is an interest in textual issues, particularly textual revision and textual indeterminacy (sometimes called new bibliography). Textual fluidity and change was the theme of the second of the two great 1980s movements. It was in 1983 that Gary Taylor and Michael Warren produced a groundbreaking textual work on *King Lear* called *The Division of the Kingdoms*.[10] This was a collection of essays by several Shakespearians, each looking at differences between the two 'good' texts we have of *Lear*, the Quarto of 1608 and the 1623 folio. While, up to that point, editors had tended to conflate good-but-different texts, *The Division of the Kingdoms* reminded readers what was known 200 years ago, but had subsequently been forgotten: that Shakespeare, a man of the theatre, did not write single, sacred, permanent texts; he wrote fluid texts that were changed, by him and by others, as historical or theatrical moments changed. Shakespeare was a reviser.

The book heralded a fascinating but untrustworthy edition of Shakespeare's *Complete Works*, the Oxford 1986 Wells and Taylor edition. Obsessed as it was with textual change and variety, this made a number of madcap decisions: to return Falstaff's name to Oldcastle, for instance, in *1 Henry IV* (which has the effect of wrenching the play from *2 Henry IV*, in which the hero is always Falstaff), or, odder still, to fill the missing metrical beats in *King John* with random seventeenth-century swear-words in order to 'return' the text to the shape it must have had. Strange as the *Complete Works* is, however, it illustrates vividly the fact that Shakespeare's plays were never set in stone. They were flexible and changeable.

There are not, unfortunately, many student-friendly books on the subject of textual revision, which still comes over as a rather dry topic on paper. Nevertheless, there are enough books and Internet sites to provide the 'tools' (facsimile reproductions of pages in quarto and folio) to enable a lecturer to explore textual revision in class. Often, anyway, revision naturally arises as part of historical context, for the ways plays have been handed down to us are historically contingent. Take the two 'good' texts of *Hamlet*. There are extracts present in the 'good' second quarto text of 1604 that are absent in the later 'good' folio text of 1623. Several have a specific historical rationale: the fact that the jokes about the drunkenness of the Danes ('they clep us drunkards . . .') are removed in the later text can be traced to the fact that King James took a Danish wife, and Danish jokes were no longer thought acceptable. What is useful to the lecturer about revision is that, as a relatively young subject, it has not yet been plumbed to the depths. That is something to stress to students. There is plenty of room for critical originality through the medium of the revision, where it really is possible to make a point that no one else has ever made before.

Strongly and directly influenced by the textual approaches of the 1980s, my 'Revenge in the Shakespearean Playhouse' course, is a comment on and a response to the education I myself received. This also introduces another more general problem besetting Shakespeare in higher education, however: the bard is institution-based and a Shakespeare course will depend on which institution is teaching him ('new' or 'old' university, for instance) and on who designed the course in question. All universities will have something roughly equating to the theoretical line, the bibliographical line or the stage-to-page line, unless, like me, they have a pick-and-mix approach gesturing towards all three. Simply skim the titles of Shakespeare modules at various universities on the Internet: all can be fitted into identifiable critical groups. 'New' universities are often more theoretical than the old. But for the course I designed, perhaps the big determiner is that, though I am teaching at a 'new' university, I was educated in two 'old' ones. Before Brookes I was a Junior Research Fellow at Merton College, Oxford (where I was also an undergraduate), and before that I was a graduate at Emmanuel College, Cambridge: so I have taught and been taught Shakespeare at two textually- and historically-motivated institutions.

Cambridge particularly had a fascination with textual uncertainty, manuscript circulation, printing-house practices, and changed and revised texts; these were themes of the M.Phil in Medieval and Renaissance Literature I took there. For the undergraduates whom I taught at Cambridge, there was a

Shakespeare paper that included both textual and theoretical questions – undergraduates usually decided whether to plump for one or the other as there was, at that period, no available 'combined' approach unless undergraduates were bold enough to come up with one themselves. Against this, was a different kind of undergraduate paper, 'Shakespeare in Performance', which examined the process Shakespeare's works underwent when being transferred from stage to page (historically and in the present). These courses belonged not just to their time, but to particular Cambridge figures. Peter Holland (now a Professor at Notre Dame University, Indiana) was a prominent stage-to-page man while I was at Cambridge, and has left his legacy in the 'performance' approach; John Kerrigan was one of the early explorers of the revision issue (indeed, he wrote one of the essays in *The Division of the Kingdoms*).

Oxford was different again. Its large baggy course is capable of accepting any approach (it has questions on all of them) whilst subscribing to none. Its main concern seems to be to stop students writing on only one or two plays – so most questions it asks are 'genre' or 'generic' questions: 'Are the tragedies really tragic?', 'Discuss the use of music and song in the plays of Shakespeare' and so forth, questions that demand a familiarity with many (and supposedly all of the) plays of Shakespeare. Nevertheless, the fact that the *Complete Works* mentioned above was completed in Oxford by editors who lived and socialized there has left the university highly revision-conscious as well.

One last influence on 'Revenge in the Shakespearean Playhouse', is, of course, my research. I have written a book, *Rehearsal from Shakespeare to Sheridan*,[11] on rehearsal historically, and the way it has affected textual change. That book and those preoccupations are, as I have said, reshaped products of my own educational background. But they are current because my generation is now writing and articulating our first books. Therefore, there will be a number of play-house-to-printing-house courses around now and for the next few years, particularly as research-led courses are useful to the department as well as the lecturer ('research-led' being one of the new buzz-words pleasing to assessors of teaching quality, the dreaded TQA).

When I look to the future, I see perhaps what I want to see. I see Shakespeare courses returning more and more to Shakespeare's writing and his theatre – because that is the direction in which scholarship is moving, and Shakespeare courses ultimately reflect what scholarship is doing. I attribute this to the conjunction of a variety of separate events and technological advances. One is practical: the discovery of the Rose theatre site, followed by the completion and opening of the new Globe theatre, has reawakened interest in the physical theatre and forced scholars to examine anew the playhouse's effect on the text. Just look at the number of books published over the last twenty years on playhouse-and-performance. Another is less tangible, being traceable to the Internet and the new possibilities it offers for, surprisingly, old-style contextual research. It is often argued that one of the reasons why America became almost entirely theory obsessed is because the universities there did not, for the most part, have access to good copyright rare-book libraries. Scholars simply could not easily *do* historical scholarship, and ended up, for that reason, taking a more theoretical approach to the literature, which required less original research. The courses such scholars created mirrored this approach: they were theory-centred rather than text-centred. The attitude is satirised by David Lodge in *Changing Places* with his American professor who has never actually read *Hamlet*, though he has seen the film and read the criticism. Now, with new subscription sites making available all

plays (Chadwyck-Healey's Literature on Line) and all rare
books (Early English Books Online), everyone, in a university
that can afford it, has access to everything printed. That will
have – and is already having – a huge knock-on effect on
research and teaching. For not only will more courses be
research-based, but students will also be able and sometimes
expected to look at texts even if they are rare or have not been
reprinted since they were first published.

One final reason for the growth of such courses is that they
meet at the interface between performance history, new historicism, and textual indeterminacy, and are therefore the
natural extension of ideas explored in the 1980s. To highlight
just a limited number of publications coming out in the play-
house-and-printing-house area now, Oxford has begun
producing a series called Oxford Shakespeare Topics, including such titles as *Shakespeare and the Drama of his Time*,[12]
Shakespeare's Dramatic Genres[13] and *Staging in Shakespeare's
Theatres*;[14] Arden Shakespeare is starting its *Shakespeare at
Stratford* series (which discusses the plays in performance) and
is accompanying its Shakespeare editions with critical works
such as *Text, Stage and Canon* and *Reading Shakespeare's
Dramatic Language*. As for text-in-context, Arden is also
launching a new series consisting of scholarly editions of non-
Shakespearian Renaissance plays, so joining Revels editions in
making plays by non-Shakespearian playwrights more easily
available. Shakespeare-in-a-broader-context seems to be where
Shakespeare *is* – or where he is going. The bigger question is
in what direction Shakespeare studies will turn after that. Will
there be a backlash return to theory? Will the context simply
be made wider and wider? Will a new approach overtake
entirely? Only time (or Time, as Shakespeare would put it) will
tell. 'So', as Ulysses said to Hector in *Troilus and Cressida*, 'to
him we leave it'.

Notes

1. Alan Sinfield, Faultlines. *Cultural Materialism and the Politics of Dissident Reading*, pp. 29–51 (Oxford University Press, 1992).

2. Germaine Greer, *The Female Eunuch* (first edition, McGibbon and Key, 1970).

3. Dympna Callaghan, *A Feminist Companion to Shakespeare* (Blackwell, 2000).

4. Andrew Gurr, *Playgoing in Shakespeare's London* (Cambridge University Press, 1996); *The Shakespearean Stage 1574–1642* (Cambridge University Press, 1992).

5. Jonathan Dollinevre, *Radical Tragedy: Religion, Ideology and Power in the Drama of Shakespeare and his Contemporaries* (Harvester, 1984).

6. Stephen Greenblatt, *Shakespearean Negotoations: The Circulation of Social Energy in Renaissance England* (Oxford University Press, 1988).

7. Stephen Greenblatt, *Renaissance Self-Fashioning* (University of Chicago Press, 1980).

8. Harold Bloom, *Shakespeare: The Invention of the Human* (Fourth Estate, 1999).

9. David Scott Kastan, *Shakespeare After Theory* (Routledge, 1999).

10. Gary Taylor and Michael Warren, *The Division of the Kingdoms* (Oxford, Clarendon Press, 1983).

11. Tiffany Stern, *Rehearsal from Shakespeare to Sheridan* (Oxford, Clarendon Press, 2000).

12. Martin Wiggins, *Shakespeare and the Drama of His Time* (Oxford University Press, 2000).

13. Lawrence Danson, *Shakespeare's Dramatic Genres* (Oxford University Press, 2000).

14. Andrew Gurr and Mariko Ichikawa, *Staging in Shakespeare's Theatres* (Oxford University Press, 2000).

CHAPTER 7

Shakespeare at the centre: the educational work of the Shakespeare Birthplace Trust

Catherine Alexander

The Trust

The title of this chapter indicates neither delusions of grandeur nor geographical significance but is an allusion to the Shakespeare Centre, the building next to Shakespeare's Birthplace in Stratford which is the base of the charitable organization known as the Shakespeare Birthplace Trust (SBT). Since I began writing this piece, 'Shakespeare at the Centre' has been borrowed as the title of the charity's Friends' magazine, but used here its function is a shorthand way of alluding to the important, worldwide role that has been played by the Trust and its employees in the provision of education and the creation of a centre of excellence for all things Shakespearian for over 150 years. This role has included the preservation of property, land, Tudor documents, and theatre records; the collection of books, paintings and artefacts; the authorship and occasional sponsorship of educational and academic publications on historical, theatrical and literary matters; the dissemination of information through lectures, courses, day schools, workshops and exhibitions; the organization of activities as diverse as a World Congress of Shakespeare and the annual celebration of Shakespeare's birthday; and supporting the teaching and learning of Shakespeare in the compulsory and voluntary sectors at home and abroad.

The Trust is also the first port of call for many with a Shakespearian enquiry – students and teachers seeking information for a school project or a reliable teaching resource, an author or publisher requiring illustrations or verification, the media reporting a new portrait of Shakespeare, pursuing a new biographical or textual conjecture, or seeking an authoritative response to yet another suggestion for the identity of the Dark Lady of the Sonnets, or a candidate for authorship. The Trust has specialists who can deal with all such enquiries and it should be evident from this far from comprehensive list that 'education' is not an isolated activity confined to the work of the four full-time and two part-time members of staff who administer and teach in the Education Department (which, as a separate entity, is a relative late-comer to a large organization) but is an integral part of the mission of the whole Trust. The educational experience of a visitor to the Shakespeare Centre may range from a tour of Shakespeare's Birthplace to postgraduate research in the Library or an assisted ancestor search in the Records Office, reading the magazine or dropping in on a temporary exhibition, as well as a more formal learning activity as part of a school, university, adult or teacher group. It follows that 'education' may be delivered by a guide in one of the Shakespeare Houses, a highly qualified Shakespearian, an historian, a visiting actor or a teacher contributing to a course. Any blurring in the account that follows between the role of the professional educators and those who work elsewhere in or for the Trust is intentional. I work part-time in the Education Department at the Trust and also lecture at the University of Birmingham, so I declare an interest as an employee and should state that just as education is implicit in the work of the Trust so is the promotion of its assets. The

Trust's properties in Stratford are major visitor attractions and it can be difficult to avoid promo-speak, but my aim has been to write an objective account and where I fail the fault is mine alone.

The Museums Department, the Records Office, the Shakespeare Houses, the Library (which alone received over 10,000 e-mail and telephone enquiries last year), the Conservationist, and even the more overtly commercial wings of the Trust have an explicit educational function. The Shakespeare Bookshop, for example, while a commercial venture, is also a unique resource for the purchase of editions, criticism and commentary, performance photographs and a broad range of teaching materials. The sense of public duty and the provision of a service that is reliable and definitive – and, where possible, free – are embedded in the Victorian origins of the Trust and its charitable status.

The Trust came into existence following the purchase, in 1847, of the building in Henley Street, Stratford, known as Shakespeare's Birthplace. The intention was to preserve the property as a national monument and the acquisition was prompted, in part, by the desire to prevent the American entrepreneur P. T. Barnum obtaining the building. The New Place estate, the site of the house to which Shakespeare retired, was purchased in 1862. The Birthplace became the nucleus for collections of books, archives, memorabilia and artefacts, and the Trust was subsequently expanded through the acquisition of Anne Hathaway's Cottage (1892), Mary Arden's House (1930), land in the Welcombe Hills once owned by Shakespeare (1930) and Hall's Croft, the home of Shakespeare's daughter Susanna and son-in-law John Hall (1949).

The three objectives of the Trust's Act of 1961 expanded the responsibilities for educational work beyond the conservation and collecting of its original inception:

a) to promote in every part of the world the appreciation and study of the plays and other works of William Shakespeare and the general advancement of Shakespearian knowledge;
b) to maintain and preserve the Shakespeare birthplace properties for the benefit of the nation;
c) to provide and maintain for the benefit of the nation a museum and a library of books, manuscripts, records of historic interest, pictures, photographs and objects of antiquity with particular but not exclusive reference to William Shakespeare, his life, works and times.

The objectives took tangible form in the provision of a lecture room, an administration area and a library in the Shakespeare Centre opened in 1964 (a project to commemorate the 400 year anniversary of Shakespeare's birth) and the additional, adjacent building of 1969 giving additional lecture halls and accommodation for the Records Office. Even the somewhat dated rhetoric of the Act, with its worthiness, its stress on 'the nation' and its intimations of bardolatry (closer to the Trust's Victorian origins than the 1960s Britain of its composition), cannot disguise an implicit educational intent. It exudes Victorian self-confidence too: there is no interrogation of or doubt about 'the benefit', but an assumption of shared cultural values and the supremacy of the national poet. The association between Shakespeare and nation, of course, has a long and persistent history. From its early manifestations in Ben Jonson's Folio verse, through the convenience of the chosen birth date (23 April) linking playwright, St George and the Order of the Garter, the chauvinistic rhetoric of the theatrical prologues of the late seventeenth century, through the damp extravaganza that was David Garrick's first Stratford Shakespeare Jubilee in 1769, to the opening of Hall's Croft in Stratford as a Festival of Britain attraction in 1951, the synonymity has been emphasized and is one that SBT, while committed to expanding its horizons, implicitly and probably inevitably affirms. While Shakespeare is the most famous playwright in the world, it cannot be denied that he was born, educated and married in Stratford-upon-Avon, and that he wrote in English.

Times change, of course, but the broad sweep of the Trust's aims, shifting perhaps toward the world view of the first objective and having accommodated new technology to provide 'electronic' Shakespeare, is delivered by departments whose responsibilities may all, however tangentially, include an educational function and whose activities frequently overlap. Such aims, history, status and structure are strengths of the institution and contribute to its reputation, but have the potential to be weaknesses too. On the one hand, the pedagogical approach and delivery of the educational work of SBT is free from the involvement of government and professional bodies and so has not suffered the external imposition of targets, assessments and evaluation, methods of recording, inspection and curricular change that has been the lot of providers of education in the public sector. It is possible, within the confines of its aims and the will of its Trustees, to resist the seemingly never-ending pressures of change and development, the pressures of competition and the debate about standards that have characterized the working conditions of those in state education. Yet charity regulations are becoming more intrusive and demanding of audit and the potential benefits of independence are only hard won through financial self-sufficiency, specifically the generation of income through visitors to the Shakespeare Houses, tourism, and the need to make educational courses and activities cost-covering or profit-making – and this can lead to insecurity and institutional timidity. The price of its valuable independence is uniquely susceptible to matters beyond the Trust's control – exchange rates, foot-and-mouth disease, the weather, terrorist threats – which may have little to do with the quality of what is on offer.

With opportunities for expansion financially limited and without pump-priming funds, there is always the danger of stagnancy or of becoming belatedly reactive rather than innovative, provincial rather than international, and for a style of least-risk, 'small c' conservatism to prevail. The temptation is difficult to resist, as the recent choice of a swan as the new logo with the strap line 'For the world's Shakespeare heritage' attests. In the face of uncertainty it is tempting to cling to the past, and Ben Jonson's association of Shakespeare and swan in his memorial verse in the 1623 Folio makes this the earliest bardic cliché. The curse of many charities – a well-intentioned enthusiastic amateurism rather than sharp professionalism – is a further hazard. Conservatism and charitable status are not, of course, inevitable weaknesses. They are an ethos and an impetus that underpin the survival of priceless historical treasures and the cultural assets that the Trust is required to conserve. Nevertheless, there is an institutional awareness of the dangers of too strong a focus on the past and a recognition of the need to be custodians of living collections and to teach or present Shakespeare for the twenty-first century rather than for some mythical golden age. While the Trust takes justifiable pride in its ownership of seventeenth- and eighteenth-century portraits of Shakespeare, for example, it is equally pleased to support modern work. Collaborations with the American Friends of SBT and the Newington-Cropsey Foundation have enabled the Shakespeare-inspired sculptures of Greg Wyatt and young artists from around the world to be displayed in the Great Garden of New Place and the Shakespeare Tree Garden in the grounds of Anne Hathaway's Cottage.

Teaching Shakespeare

If vulnerability to market forces is one of the unique tensions implicit in the work of the Trust that can manifest itself in the age-old culture clash between education and commerce, idealism and pragmatism, then there are others that will be familiar to those who work in more conventional educational establishments. Is teaching 'Shakespeare' a matter of teaching history? The Trust's ownership of Shakespeare's Birthplace, his mother's house, his wife's family home, his retirement home, his son-in-law's house, contemporary artefacts, and roughly half of the surviving Shakespeare documents afford unrivalled opportunities to do so. Or is teaching 'Shakespeare' a question of literature? The Trust's collection of early printed books includes three first Folios, six second Folios, one third Folio and four fourth Folios in addition to Quartos and subsequent editions. 'Shakespeare' may be the study of performance and, again, a unique picture collection arranged by play and the Royal Shakespeare Company archive offers unrivalled potential. Or is teaching 'Shakespeare' some branch of cultural studies? Many school groups roam the streets of Stratford with clipboards and questionnaires asking pedestrians about tourism and travel rather than Shakespeare, and a group of adults outside the Birthplace recently was pursuing clues for a Stratford hotel's Murder and Mystery Weekend with only the most peripheral Shakespeare connections. Should the department teach 'Shakespeare' (however defined) as a subject or is method more important? Even with broad agreement that text in/and performance is the major focus of the department's work, there remain important questions of delivery. Until very recently one could confidently offer, at school level, programmes that focused closely on language, narrative or the exploration of character, and that used practical or active methods of delivery.[1] These ways of accessing texts are beginning to take second place to the interest in contexts, a shift driven by changes in curriculum and assessment which are themselves influenced by watered-down literary theory, reception studies, an awareness of issues of race and gender, the disappearance of the certainties of liberal humanism, and the modular delivery of many courses.

Certainly, as the historical and cultural distance between text and taught increases and, arguably, as the focus on style of delivery rather than substance ('skills' rather than knowledge) intensifies in education generally, there is a case that can be made for a departmental shift away from its traditional strengths of textual knowledge and expertise towards pedagogy. Colleagues throughout the education world will be familiar with these debates and with their manifestations in the discussions, which are beginning to sideline them and have become so dominant, about fundraising, promotion and publicity. It would be true to say that the philosophical, pedagogical, and increasingly the commercial relationships between literature and history have not been fully explored by the department. In many cases, of course, the answers to questions about delivery are provided by the specific needs of the very broad audiences that constitute the Trust's users. It is they who determine, in part, whether Shakespeare is offered as literature, history, cultural icon, text or performance and, particularly in work undertaken with groups of teachers, whether the focus is on 'what' or 'how'. Requests can be very detailed. Recently the Head of English at a Bristol sixth-form college made contact asking for help with a group of students 'working with the AQA Specification (A). They need to study *Othello*, particularly in relation to how the text has been interpreted by other readers. I am taking this to include the students themselves, literary critics and directors and actors. I am hoping that you could give them an overview of this, or focus on some selected specific readings.' A tall order perhaps for an hour and a half session, and a far cry from the type of lecture request that the Education Department was receiving until very recently, but certainly not a difficult one to respond to. The picture collection, the RSC archive, the library holdings, the *Othello* pages in the Study Shakespeare section of the Trust's website (*www.shakespeare.org.uk*) provide ample and unique resources.

A noticeable trend, closely connected to the shift towards context, and prompted perhaps by the reassessments of great men or great ages that accompanied the millennium, is the revival of interest in Shakespeare's biography. Possibly the interest had never quite gone away and it is the revisionist, critical spirit of the age and shift of critical and theoretical standpoints that has enabled the focus to move from the works to the life. Certainly, the present attention paid to the man falls far short of the hagiography that characterized earlier biographies. SBT has been able to respond to this interest in 'Shakespeare the Man' through its holdings of primary and secondary materials, the presentation of the properties and through its teaching programmes.

Recent academic and popular biographies such as Katherine Duncan-Jones's *Ungentle Shakespeare: Scenes from his Life* (The Arden Shakespeare, 2001), Stanley Wells's *Shakespeare: The Poet and His Plays* (Methuen, 2001, a revision of *Shakespeare: A Dramatic Life* published by Sinclair-Stevenson in 1994), Anthony Holden's *William Shakespeare: his Life and Work* (Little, Brown and Company, 1999), and Park Honan's *Shakespeare: A Life* (Oxford University Press, 1998) all made use of the resources and expertise of the Records Office and the Library. Many of the requests for information about Shakespeare the Man come from teachers, pupils and students, by letter, phone or, increasingly, e-mail, and are triggered by the need to find reliable and authoritative material for project work. The Trust provides 'hard text' packs – *William Shakespeare: His Life and Background* – which include a booklet of biographical information, postcards of portraits of Shakespeare and the Stratford properties associated with him, A4-sized facsimiles of early maps of London and Stratford, and documents (Shakespeare's baptism and burial entries in the parish records, his marriage licence bond, Richard Quiney's letter to Shakespeare, part of his will) in addition to contextual and largely contemporary illustrations of Stratford, Queen Elizabeth and King James, a page from Holinshed's *Chronicles*, and prefatory material from the First Folio.

Some of the material in the pack is replicated from the permanent exhibition in the Visitors' Centre of Shakespeare's Birthplace and is also available in the 'About Shakespeare' section of the Trust's website, where it is supplemented by the 'Frequently Asked Questions' pages. Sixty or so answers, written by specialists from every department, attempt to deal with the most common enquiries. The 'Shakespeare's Life' answers cover, for example, 'What sort of education did Shakespeare have?', 'Why did Shakespeare leave his wife his "second best" bed?' and 'Was Shakespeare gay?' The section on 'The Works' is more quantitative than critical or descriptive, dealing with 'What is the longest play?' and 'Which is the longest female role?' 'Performance' deals largely with the theatre of Shakespeare's day and 'Elizabethan England' covers social history: questions about diet and life-style, 'How tall were people in Shakespeare's day?' and the fascinating 'What were the toilet facilities like in Shakespeare's day?'

Almost all the study courses that are run for universities will begin with an illustrated 'Shakespeare and Stratford' or 'Shakespeare's Life and Times' lecture with a biographical focus, to underpin the work of the week with a contextualized foundation; course members will invariably also visit the Birthplace. The popularity of these activities may seem surprising, teetering as they do on the verges of bardolatry and suspect assumptions about accessing the works through the man (or, even more irritatingly, the man through the works), but a carefully prepared presentation of life in a sixteenth-century market town and its most famous resident can puncture myth, reduce the risk of a Stratford visit becoming a pilgrimage, and may inform if not the plays then something of the age of their composition and reception. The ambience of the Birthplace is unreverential and some way removed from presenting a romanticized picture of either Shakespeare or the mythical golden age he has been thought, by some, to inhabit. The major re-display of the interior of the building (formally opened in 2000 by Dame Judi Dench and Michael Williams) with its brightly coloured replica wall-hangings and the re-creation of John Shakespeare's leather workshops, surprises many of its half a million annual visitors who may arrive with black and white, half-timbered expectations. It is vivid and conveys a sense of a living, working house which is some distance from the gloomy, nineteenth-century presentation, dominated by a bust of Shakespeare, where many writers and actors paid homage, including Keats, Dickens, Tennyson, Longfellow, Twain, Irving and Terry, and Hardy.

The quantity of visitors, and the expectation of many of a speedy progression with photo opportunities, make the use of the Birthplace itself as a teaching resource impractical. Much more accessible and amenable for school groups is Mary Arden's House, the farmhouse at Wilmcote, a couple of miles outside Stratford, that was the home of Shakespeare's mother. This is a fine facility for cross-curricular work with primary school classes, affording opportunities for the study of more broad-based Tudor social and agricultural history than the

Stratford Shakespeare Houses allows. The collections of rare breeds of cattle and farm machinery, the falconry displays and the re-created interior of the farmhouse lend themselves to practical and experiential approaches to learning. Adult visitors too are encouraged to attend the special events that celebrate the farming year. It is a further example of the remarkable range of the Trust's educational work, and there is something delightful in discovering that the care that is given, say, to the purchase of a late sixteenth-century physic box for the display of medical artefacts at Hall's Croft (John Hall, Shakespeare's son-in-law, was a physician) is also afforded to the acquisition of a pair of oxen to work the land at Mary Arden's House. It is evidence too of the wide range of expertise that characterizes the Trust.

If debate about *what* is done is familiar to many (and I shall be returning to some of our non-biographical provision) then equally familiar, I suspect, will be debate about the best use of resources. The physical resources of the Trust are priceless and need conservation, preservation and presentation. They are expensive to maintain and display to the public. An increasing amount of time is spent in promotion and appeals (legacies, bequests, 'adopting' treasures, membership drives for Friends) and heads of department have a fundraising function in their job descriptions. The staff feel stretched and react with varying degrees of enthusiasm to the need to make their work profitable. But financial imperatives aside, there is professional difficulty for very small departments in trying to maintain an individual identity while at the same time responding to diverse users' needs and, in the attempt to be all-encompassing, the associated danger of dissipating expertise and becoming unfocused. The small and highly specialized academic departments have gone some way towards resolving this dilemma by working cooperatively with each other and with external providers to maintain standards and to reach larger audiences through professional collaboration. Internally, cooperation is evident in the development of the website and in the temporary exhibitions held in the foyer of the Centre. 'Shakespeare: A Man of the Millennium' with sections on 'Commemorations', 'Politics and Propaganda', 'Images', 'Shakespeare's Lives' and 'International Reworkings of Texts', and a display of artefacts was the product of collaboration between all the academic departments. The recent exhibition, 'The Children's Midsummer Night's Dream' – a display of costumes, film stills, commentary and text that accompanied the national launch of the film – was the product of internal cooperation between the Education and Museums Departments, and external cooperation with Sands Films and the Stratford Picture House (the local cinema).

A school group visiting the Centre mainly for a lecture prior to a theatre visit or for classes or workshops to supplement and support its A-Level studies will have its principal contact with a member of the education team, but may also benefit from the expertise of other departments. A group that visits annually from Edinburgh, for example, always requests some input from the Library, having discovered how inspirational it can be to have a hands-on (and white-gloved) encounter with a First Folio. Such an experience, followed up with a simple comparison between their school Shakespeare study text and the original, is an early taste for many of basic bibliography, and a revelation of editorial intervention.

A more experienced group of visitors, the students working on an eighteenth-century Shakespeare module at the University of Cambridge Shakespeare Summer School, spent time in the Education Department in July 2001 but also looked at eighteenth-century texts, promptbooks, illustrations and criticism in the Library and worked on primary materials concerning the 1769 Stratford Jubilee (David Garrick's letters, Town Council Documents, and first-hand accounts) in the Records Office. Again, the unmediated encounter with unique primary source material can be exciting and inspirational and, for some, the first insight into research method. Such an opportunity, however, is very labour intensive and expensive for a relatively small group, and it may be difficult to sustain such work in the future.

There is less collaborative working within the Education Department itself than colleagues in other sectors might expect. The staff bring a range of expertise to their work at the Trust: experience in teaching and management in primary, secondary and higher education and in teacher training and with the Royal Shakespeare Company, and in records of research and publication in education and in Shakespeare study. Yet within the Trust their areas of responsibility are discrete (broadly speaking, university courses, schools and teachers, lifelong learners, and publishing), and while they frequently contribute to and teach on each other's programmes, their work is remarkably autonomous. This reflects the management of resources as much as organizational policy, and also influences the increasing shift of role away from that of hands-on teachers and towards that of project or programme directors, advisers or contributors of expertise in partnerships with other providers, initiated from within or without the Trust.

Educational Partnerships

The most prominent external partnerships are with the other pillars of Stratford Shakespeare: the Royal Shakespeare Company and the Shakespeare Institute (the Stratford-based postgraduate outpost of the University of Birmingham). The overlap of personnel and expertise is such that some users may be unaware of the distinctions. Trust staff teach on the MA and Diploma courses of the Institute and lecture there, and each year up to 40 universities, from all over the world, will send groups of undergraduates and postgraduates to the Centre for study courses on 'Shakespeare in Performance' jointly run by the Trust and the Shakespeare Institute. In the course of a long week students may see seven productions by the RSC (not exclusively Shakespeare: there may be modern plays at The Other Place and a Jacobean or eighteenth-century play at The Swan), receive pre-performance lectures from the Trust and Institute staff, and have post-performance discussions with lecturers, actors and theatre staff. Many students have encountered Shakespeare on film and video and may, through media or cultural studies, have acquired a critical language and an analytical objectivity for such an approach. Few students, however, have equal experience of live performance or have acquired the techniques or vocabulary to describe, discuss or record it. And while many will speak knowingly of the theories of Bertolt Brecht or Mikhail Bakhtin, this can be poor preparation for an encounter with leading actors and theatre practitioners as diverse as fight directors, wig makers, company managers, designers or musicians.

Some groups, particularly from universities in countries where the pedagogical style concentrates on one-way instruction rather than shared discussion, need confidence-building activities to engage in effective debate; most need sessions on performance history, the translation of text from page to stage, and aesthetic effect; almost all need help to define the parameters of a discussion of performance and the appropriateness of some areas of debate. Some groups can become unexpectedly gauche and even ill-mannered when encountering a live performer. Asking a leading actor about her personal relationship with a co-star is out, asking about the development of professional relationships during the rehearsal process is in. The tripartite partnership affords opportunities to respond to the individual needs and experiences of diverse student groups.

The association with the theatre is long established and takes many forms. At its most practical and mundane, SBT provides occasional rehearsal space. Most RSC programmes include notes on Shakespeare, the play and its performance written by SBT staff, and many use illustrations from its archives. The *Players of Shakespeare* series of Cambridge University Press (jointly edited by Robert Smallwood, the Director of Education at SBT until 2001, and Russell Jackson of the Shakespeare Institute) developed from the working relationship with RSC actors. The new *Shakespeare at Stratford* series from the Arden Shakespeare in association with the Shakespeare Birthplace Trust, under the general editorship of Robert Smallwood, has a focus on performances at the Stratford theatres from 1945 onwards, and draws on the RSC archive at the Trust.[2] Further collaboration is evident in the exhibition that was devised by the RSC Curator and the Trust's Education Department to accompany the 2001 production of Peter Barnes's new play *Jubilee* in The Swan Theatre (and which was subsequently displayed at the Heritage Centre in Lichfield). The play considered David Garrick's contribution to the Shakespeare Industry, triggered by his 1769 Stratford Shakespeare Jubilee, and the exhibition drew on holdings from the Trust's Library, Records Office and Museums Department, the RSC's picture collection, and the skills of the Trust's photographer.

Such fruitful collaborations rely on professional relationships that have been built up over many years and may therefore be vulnerable to changes of personnel and, indeed, policy changes by one of the partners. There is some concern in Stratford at the time of writing (December 2001) about RSC plans that may reduce the repertoire and the number of playing spaces and, in the short term at least, subsequently reduce the number of groups who visit Stratford for study courses and who may not be prepared to make long, expensive journeys for just two or three Shakespeare plays. Equally vulnerable is the RSC annual summer school, co-directed by the head of the Shakespeare Institute and the head of the Education Department at the Trust, and a feature of the Stratford summer, attracting hundreds of teachers and enthusiasts, for 54 years. SBT is clearly susceptible, financially and professionally, to such changes and, being aware of the potential dangers of an over-reliance on a few cooperative associations, seeks new partners to further its mission. It has worked with Globe Education and Film Education, for example, and currently collaborates with the English Association in jointly running an open-access undergraduate 'Shakespeare for Students' course and in hosting teachers' courses. Long-standing collaboration with the Central Bureau of the British Council has linked the Trust's expertise with the needs of teachers from across Europe in a series of Stratford-based courses on the teaching of Shakespeare. Teachers from even further afield visit the Centre for courses jointly run with the International Shakespeare Association. Yet the presence of the theatre must be acknowledged as one of the attractions of a Stratford-based course, as must the Education Department's strengths in performance studies, and so it remains to be seen if alternative attractions can compensate for any diminution in the RSC's work.

Outreach

While collaborative working is one way of maximizing resources and skills, a parallel development has been in the quantity of outreach work that is undertaken. Not only can larger audiences be addressed through this mode of working, thus fulfilling the first of the Trust's aims, but it is frequently of financial benefit to hosts who find the costs, in time and transport, of a Stratford visit prohibitive. It has not been unknown for a lecture on an A-Level play to be delivered to an audience of 600 assembled in a major city. It is easier and cheaper to organize such a gathering in Manchester, say, where students from a number of schools and colleges can arrange their own transport, than to bus such numbers to Stratford. More common has been a lecture to 150 as part of an English Association A-Level conference, or to a single school or college group. After a brief lull while teachers got to grips with the demands of the new A-Level specifications, discovering what they could provide through their own classes and identifying areas where external support was required, this type of work is on the increase, although the pattern of work is shifting and not yet settled. With the 'old' A-level the bulk of lecture requests came at the end of the autumn term and at late spring revision time. The department could plan and present study days, at home or away, devoted to a specific play at predictable moments throughout the academic year with the expectation of attracting students from half a dozen schools. New, modular A-levels are challenging such certainties.

Outreach is not confined to the direct delivery of secondary education. 'The *Cymbeline* Project' was undertaken in conjunction with a Hertfordshire primary school, linking with its work at Key Stage Two and fulfilling and enhancing the demands of the National Literacy Strategy. The project involved text work, creative writing, art and music and ultimately involved all the pupils in Years 5 and 6. A more wide-ranging and ambitious example of outreach was the Millennium Link Project of the year 2000, involving schools, colleges and professional and amateur theatre groups throughout the world who were encouraged to undertake a Shake-speare-inspired performance, record it in a range of media and then deposit the records in a permanent archive at the Shake-speare Centre.

Invitations to work abroad and lecture at European univer-sities are accepted when they can be fitted into busy schedules and, in addition to fulfilling the Trust's remit, allow for the strengthening of professional Shakespearian relationships and keep staff up-to-date, in a very practical way, with worldwide trends of scholarship.

Outreach is also achieved by the more conventional method of publishing, both in traditional hard text and by electronic means. As with other areas of the department's work, the pub-lishing role takes three forms: advisory, contributory, and initiatory. Education staff advise on the content and style of Shakespeare books for children and collaborate with educa-tional publishers on editions and study material.[3] They write for learned journals and contribute to major Shakespeare pub-lications.[4] They edit and commission new work.[5] The quarterly magazine provides an opportunity to explain the work of the Trust to a worldwide audience and to respond promptly in print to Shakespeare discoveries and debate.

It is, however, the website that reaches the largest audience, and is a Trust activity that reflects the work of the whole insti-tution and has contributions from every department. It has grown exponentially, from origins that did little more than communicate in electronic form material that already existed in hard text: lists of collections, diaries of activities, descrip-tions of departmental roles, information for visitors. Authoritative accounts of Shakespeare's life and times were added and illustrated study materials, broadly targeted at A-level and college students, appended. The aim has been to provide reliability, avoiding speculation, and the site is currently being redesigned to make it more accessible to users who do not, of course, understand the internal departmental organization of the Trust, and who need clearer navigational aids to make the best use of the resources it offers. It is planned to add to the study materials with further pages devoted to single plays, and one that focuses on Shakespeare's language (a subject due for a revival of interest if public debate and publishers' lists are any guide) and, looking further ahead, to consider a more interactive use of the site to exploit the possibilities of distance learning.

What else of the future? An area of work that continues to grow and is mercifully free of curricular pressures is the provision made for lifelong learners. Lunchtime lectures, study days and weekly leisure courses cater for the interests of an increasing number of adults who have the time and the desire to enhance their historical and literary knowledge of Shakespeare. So many adult classes offered by university and college Continuing Studies departments are now only available as part of a certificated or examined (and frequently expensive) extended course that the Trust's shorter and more convenient study opportunities are immensely popular. Such work is enjoyed by staff too – it affords the chance to share skills, research and special interests that do not necessarily have an outlet in courses that are tied to a syllabus or specific user needs. A lunchtime lecture might be on images of Shakespeare, the theatrical work of Bram Stoker, the supernatural in Shakespeare's plays, the First Folio or the Shakespeare documents in the Records Office, and may be delivered by a member of staff from any of the academic departments. Such work is rewarding too because of the enthusiasm and in many cases the varied and long experiences of the audiences. Some participants will have memories of Shakespeare in performance from the 1930s onwards, and such first-hand experience can help reconstruct the presentation and reception of a play and enhance the more conventional academic resources of promptbook, production photographs and reviews.

The only restrictions to the growth of such work, and indeed to the other functions of the Education Department, are time pressures on staff and financial ones. The work can seem relentless without the relief afforded by the shape of the academic year. Work with schools may take place largely between September and July, but teachers' courses tend to be vacation-based. Most of the university study courses occur between April and October, adult work and publishing is year-round, and dominating much of what is done are the shifting performance schedules of the RSC. Responding to all these needs leaves little time for the research and development that is acknowledged to be necessary if new ideas are to be initiated to 'promote in every part of the world the appreciation and study of the works of William Shakespeare and the general advancement of Shakespearian knowledge.' With only four teaching staff (two of them part-time) expansion is not an option. There may be changes of emphases, new partnerships, a more hard-headed business approach and more energy devoted to promotion and sponsorship, but the overall quantity of work is likely to remain the same. A new Head of Department has been in place since November 2001, and he is keen to promote activities that will generate excitement about Shakespeare's skills. This may lead to more advisory work and less hands-on teaching, or there may be a better service to local schools or a commitment to the inner-city. There may be a greater use of the Shakespeare Houses as a teaching resource, or the extension of worldwide initiatives. Whatever happens, Shakespeare will remain central to the work of the Department, and such a singleness of focus should preserve the unique nature of the educational provision.

Notes

1. See, for example, Rex Gibson's essays '"O, what learning is!" Pedagogy and the afterlife of *Romeo and Juliet*' and 'Narrative approaches to Shakespeare: active storytelling in schools' in *Shakespeare Survey* 49 and *Shakespeare Survey* 53, and the recommended activities in many school editions of Shakespeare.

2. Gillian Day, *Shakespeare at Stratford: King Richard III* (2002); Miriam Gilbert, *Shakespeare at Stratford: The Merchant of Venice* (2002); Patricia E. Tatspaugh, *Shakespeare at Stratford: The Winter's Tale* (2002). All London: Thomson Learning.

3. See, for example, Teresa O'Connor's Film Education study packs and Rebecca Flynn's selections of slides, with commentaries, of RSC productions.

4. Catherine Alexander and Paul Edmondson both contributed entries to *The Oxford Companion to Shakespeare*, ed. Dobson and Wells (Oxford University Press, 2002).

5. See, for example, *Shakespeare and Race* (Cambridge University Press, 2000) and *Shakespeare and Sexuality* (Cambridge University Press, 2001) both edited by Catherine Alexander and Stanley Wells.

Index